Learn Smart

Smart

STRATEGIES TO SUCCEED IN SCHOOL AND LIFE

The staff of Emond Montgomery Publications Limited
dedicates this book to the memory of our dear
friend and colleague, Dayne Ogilvie.

Be curious, not judgmental.

—*Walt Whitman*

Learn Smart

STRATEGIES TO SUCCEED IN SCHOOL AND LIFE

JESSICA PEGIS, GENERAL EDITOR

MARC EMOND
Social Sciences and Humanities Teacher
SOLA-School of Liberal Arts
Toronto, Ontario

PAUL GALPERN
Queen Elizabeth District High School
Keewatin-Patricia District School Board
Sioux Lookout, Ontario

GILLIAN HALL
Coordinator of Special Education
JW Singleton Centre
Halton District School Board

CHRISTEL KIRSTEIN
ESL/Special Education Resource Teacher
White Oaks Secondary School
Halton District School Board

LAURA LEESTI
Curriculum Consultant
Instruction and Assessment for Literacy Learning K-12
York Region District School Board

GLENYS REITHER
ESL/Special Education Resource Teacher
White Oaks Secondary School
Halton District School Board

emp

2007
EMOND MONTGOMERY PUBLICATIONS
TORONTO, CANADA

Emond Montgomery Publications Limited
60 Shaftesbury Avenue
Toronto ON M4T 1A3
http://www.emp.ca/school

Printed in Canada.
Reprinted October 2012.

We acknowledge the financial support of the Government of Canada through the Canada Book Fund for our publishing activities.

Publisher
Anthony Rezek

Sales & marketing supervisor
Lindsay Sutherland

Editorial assistant
Eunice Hamilton

Production editor, copy editor, & image researcher
Francine Geraci

Permissions editor
Jane Affleck

Additional writing
Chelsea Donaldson
Derek Grant
Dayne Ogilvie
Jay Somerset

Illustrations
Darren Hick
Shani Sohn
Tara Wells

Cover design & interior design
Shani Sohn

Compositors
Shani Sohn
Tara Wells

Proofreader
David Handelsman

Indexer
Paula Pike

Production coordinator
Jim Lyons

Library and Archives Canada Cataloguing in Publication

Learn smart : strategies to succeed in school and life / Jessica Pegis, general editor ; Marc Emond ... [et al.].

Includes index.
ISBN 978-1-55239-169-3

    1. Learning strategies—Textbooks.   2. Study skills—Textbooks.   3. Life skills—Textbooks.   I. Pegis, Jessica II. Emond, Marc

LB1060.L42 2007   373.13028'1   C2007-902152-2

Advisory Panel

Emond Montgomery Publications Limited would like to thank the following reviewers and advisers for their contributions to the development of *Learn Smart: Strategies to Succeed in School and Life.*

Kellie Casey-Shaw
Simcoe County District School Board

Kathleen Currie
School of Liberal Arts
Toronto, Ontario

Sandi Della Vedova
Toronto District School Board

Pat Harrison
Social Studies Consultant, Winnipeg
1 School Division

Jan Haskings-Winner
Ontario Institute for Studies in Education
University of Toronto
Toronto District School Board

Chris Kennedy
Principal, Riverside Secondary School,
Coquitlam District #43, British Columbia

Aileen MacInnes
York District School Board

Teresa Miceli
Cardinal Carter Academy for the Arts,
Toronto District School Board

Stacy Shepley
Branksome Hall
Toronto, Ontario

Lana Thompson
Simcoe County District School Board

CONTENTS

SKILLS WORKSHOPS

WELCOME TO *LEARN SMART!*

Learn Smart is your guide to learning. It will help you build your strengths, manage your challenges, practise your skills, and boost your self-confidence in a variety of settings. The learning you do in this course isn't just for school—it's for life. But first, here's a guide to getting around the book.

Open It Up

Part openers show you what you are expected to learn in that section of the book. Together, all four parts of *Learn Smart* make up the expectations for your learning strategies course.

Collect the Evidence

You'll start a learning strategies portfolio in Chapter 1. Every time you see this icon, add your work to your portfolio. Look at it often to see how far you've come.

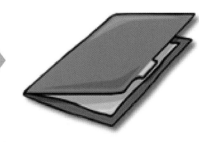

Get Support

When you see this icon, ask your teacher for a line master to help you complete the activity.

Get the Meaning

Find the meaning of bolded words in the margin glossary.

learn smart
to learn in a way that suits you; to maximize your strengths and manage your challenges

Get Wise

These are quotes to inspire and think about. They may help you think in different ways about learning.

WISE WORDS

It's not how smart you are, but how you are smart.

Use the Pictures

Learn Smart uses lots of visuals to convey information. You're on the right track if you look at the pictures first.

Type of Communication		What You Do
Aggressive communication		• Raise your voice • Blame • Call names • Force or threaten
Passive communication		• Speak quietly • Don't say what need or how yo • Feel angry insid
		• Speak confidently • Ask for what you w politely • Show that you understand how other person f

Do you eat popcorn at the movies?

Number of People

20
15
10
5
0

Said YES   Said NO

Inside the bloodstream of a healthy person, immune cells are busy getting rid of any invaders they find.

Surf the Web

This icon points out additional Web sites of interest available at www.emp.ca/ls.

Read On

These activities accompany the 20 practice texts in *Learn Smart*. They

- help you connect your reading to what you already know
- give you strategies for reading the text
- let you check your understanding.

Connect the Text

■ People need relationships, but sometimes they turn sour. Jot down five characteristics of a healthy relationship. It can be any kind of relationship—not just a romantic one.

Reading Strategy

These words and phrases are all from the article below. What might this article be about?

addicted   married
Dear Desperate

Read for Meaning

1. Look again at the five-point list you created under Connect the Text. For each point, find a quotation from the article to prove that an unhealthy relationship is the exact opposite of a healthy one.
2. Quote a word from the article that indicates that Desperate and his girlfriend need to be together all the time.
3. Quote a phrase from the article that proves that Desperate is very unhappy.

This icon means that there are multiple-choice questions you can do instead of these activities.

Write On

These activities also accompany the practice texts and help you brush up on your writing skills.

Sharpen Your Writer's Craft

1. In the first sentence of the article, suggest another word for "violent."
2. Explain why the word "spotters," in paragraph 1, is in quotation marks.
3. Why does paragraph 5 begin with an incomplete sentence? With a question?
4. How does the picture of the hailstones support the information that you read in the text?

Get the Skill

These workshops are like having your own tutor. They teach you skills that are necessary for school and for life. And you get to figure out how that skill helps you.

SKILLS WORKSHOP

How to Listen—Even When It's Not Your Style

Listening seems to come more naturally to some people than to others. However, there are ways to improve your listening ability. Practise the following activities several times and watch your listening curve go up and up.

Listening Tips

1. "Did You Get That?"
In this game, your teacher or another student reads something out loud. It could be a

2. Listen and Paraphrase

Work with a partner to take turns reading some text aloud. You can choose from the articles in Part 2, which starts on page 31, or some other text you feel comfortable reading. Read only one paragraph at a time. Your partner must paraphrase what you have read. (Paraphrasing means stating the information in your own words.) Then, switch places with your partner.

3. Ask a Question

Some people just naturally tune out when

Jump In

These activities give you the chance to jump in and practise what you are learning. It could be anything from a math problem to a locker makeover!

Jump In

1. Movies with motion-capture are often very expensive to make. Examine these box office figures for movies that have used motion-capture animation:

Mo-Cap at the Box Office

Movie	Year Released	Estimated Movie Budget*	Box Office Ticket Sales*
Star Wars: Episode 1—The Phantom Menace	1999	$115 000 000	$922 379 000
Lord of the Rings: The Fellowship of the Ring	2001	$109 000 000	$860 700 000
The Polar Express	2004	$170 000 000	$274 871 234

* All amounts shown in US dollars.

Get the Power

These activities give you the chance to work in a team. With other students, you will

- use the skills of teamwork
- identify the benefits of teamwork
- identify actions, attitudes, and resources that help you to learn and grow.

Empower Yourself

Money Management

The London Police Service started using propane-fuelled cars because they wanted to save money. Saving and managing money is important to large organizations like a police force, hospital, or school. Saving money is also important to individuals.

1. As a class, try to brainstorm all the things students your age need and want money for. Keep track of the list on a chalkboard or sheet of chart paper.
2. Next, as a class, brainstorm all the ways in which students your age can get money.
3. In a group of two to five students, consider the question: If you had an unlimited supply of money, what would you do? Each person in the group should contribute three ideas. Make a list of the top five ideas from group members. Keep your ideas handy. In Chapter 8, you will be asked to revisit this question.

Sum It Up

Use the chapter summaries in chapters 1, 2, 8, 9, and 10 to find the important ideas and to get page references for more information.

This chapter introduced you to the following ideas:

- Knowing yourself—your interests, abilities, and preferred learning style—is the first step in learning how to learn smart.
- Your brain has a creative side and an analytic side. Most people feel they are more creative or more analytic.
- There are nine intelligences, or "smarts." Most people have more than one kind of smarts. You can have one kind of smarts or a combination.
- There are three main learning styles. These are described on page 8. Use your preferred style to learn smart.
- Listening is something everyone needs to do. You can improve your listening skills by using the strategies described on page 9.
- You can help to create interest and motivation even when you are bored or turned off. Find those tips on pages 11-12.

PART 1
Learn It, Don't Sweat It

In this section of *Learn Smart*, you will have the opportunity to

- identify your interests and abilities
- get to know your "smarts" and learning style and their role in learning
- make the most of your learning style in different situations
- start a portfolio to keep a "profile of you" and evidence of your learning
- sharpen your personal management skills

- manage your time and your personal space
- set goals
- learn to use study skills effectively
- increase your interest and motivation in learning better
- overcome barriers to learning
- identify healthy lifestyle choices that support learning and growth

CHAPTER 1

It's Your Style

Project You

Daniel has just joined a growing online community. This morning he is about to create a personal profile. "Wow, it really is all about me," Daniel chuckles as he starts answering questions about his personal qualities and interests.

Daniel is hoping to connect with other young people like him—people who have similar qualities and who enjoy similar activities.

WISE WORDS

It's not how smart you are, but how you are smart.

What kind of person is Daniel? Do you think he is shy or outgoing? What qualities do you think he might be looking for in other people?

The Importance of Knowing Yourself

Knowing yourself is the first step in connecting with new people. It's also a key step in learning how to **learn smart**. When you understand your own qualities and abilities, you can use the information to make the most of your abilities. That information can also help you manage your personal challenges.

Most successful people have learned how to do this. They know they can't be good at everything, but they can be good at being themselves.

learn smart
to learn in a way that suits you; to maximize your strengths and manage your challenges

Starting Your Portfolio

During your **learning strategies** course, you will be recording a lot of information about yourself and for yourself. Whenever you see this icon, be sure to place your completed information in your portfolio. Don't forget to review your portfolio regularly. It will show you where you have been and the progress you've been making—evidence of your learning.

learning strategies
ways to help you learn more easily and effectively at school and throughout life

Jump In

1. a) Take a few minutes to think of words or phrases that describe you. Write these on a blank piece of paper. (You can do this activity with a partner.) Keep this page in front of you.

   b) On **Line Master 1-1: My Brand**, write the letters of your name down one column. From your page of words, find those words that start with the letters of your name. If you don't have a word that starts with the right letter, use a **thesaurus** to find one. Here is one example using the first letter of Daniel's name.

thesaurus
a dictionary of synonyms and antonyms

Letters of your name	Word starting with that letter that describes you	Why you chose this word
D	Daring	Sometimes I am daring. I think daring people change the world.

   c) Using paper and art supplies provided by your teacher, make a "My Brand" poster advertising your qualities. Use the one shown here as inspiration. Place your completed poster in your portfolio.

   d) Alternative to activity 1c): Create an e-mail signature tag out of your name. There are many Web sites that show you how to do this—your teacher will share some of them with you. Print your tag and use it to make a poster or graphic that describes you.

2. Select one personal quality you possess (e.g., thoughtfulness, **resilience**, stubbornness) that has helped you in the past at school or in life.

   a) In what situation did it help you?

   b) How did it help you?

3. Give Daniel some tips on Internet safety and online communities. Send it to him in an e-mail.

C

Daring
Alert
Never boring
Inspired
Enjoys graphic design
Life of the party

resilience
the ability to bounce back from difficulties

Building a Personal Profile

Your personal qualities are just one part of you. You also have abilities and interests. Together, your personal qualities, abilities, and interests give a fairly well-rounded picture of you.

Your Interests

What you're interested in tells people a lot about you. What really interests and excites you? What activities are so interesting they cause you to lose track of time? Are there issues that you feel strongly about? What are they? Why do they interest you so much?

Here's an exercise to do by yourself or with a partner. All you need is paper and a pencil. Write down all those activities that you enjoy doing or that interest you—for example, playing sports, hanging out with friends, or going to your part-time job. Be totally honest, and don't worry if some of the activities or interests seem impractical.

The purpose of this exercise is to help you identify your passion. Following your passion can be applied to many areas of life.

Jump In

1. a) This is a whole-class activity. Your teacher will distribute **Line Master 1-2: Bingo! V-e-r-y Interesting**. Your task is to find people that match the interests listed on your bingo card. Once you have a completed row (see illustration below), you call out "Bingo!"

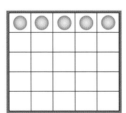 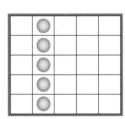 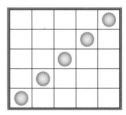

2. What are you interested in? It can be anything. It doesn't have to be a school subject, but it can be. In a group of two to five students, brainstorm some of your interests. Some examples include hobbies or favourite things to do by yourself or with your friends. Use **Line Master 1-3: Interests Inventory** to record your ideas individually.

Interests in School	Interests Outside School

Place your completed chart in your portfolio.

Your Amazing Brain

You already know whether you're right- or left-handed. It turns out that your brain also has an analytic and a creative side.

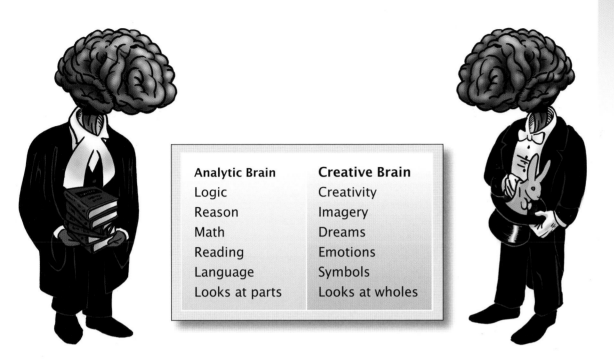

Analytic Brain	Creative Brain
Logic	Creativity
Reason	Imagery
Math	Dreams
Reading	Emotions
Language	Symbols
Looks at parts	Looks at wholes

Analytic and creative thinking

Your creative brain controls your creative, dreamy side. Take a moment to remember what it feels like when you let your mind drift. Maybe you pause to notice the way something appears in nature. Or perhaps you remember a few bars of music. Notice how one thing flows into the other. At that moment, you are using your creative brain.

Now think back to a time when you had to do a math problem or write an essay. Your mind is working in a completely different way. You are in analytic mode. You are using **reason** to solve the math problem. Maybe you are breaking it down into its parts. You may be using lots of "if … then" statements, as in, "Okay, if 3x + 4 = 16, then x = 4," or "If that guy was such a bad leader, then why did he stay in power?"

Most people feel that they are mostly creative or mostly analytical. However, it is certainly possible to develop both kinds of brain power. *Learn Smart* includes lots of activities to help you do that.

reason
understanding an idea because of another idea

Jump In

Are you mostly analytic or mostly creative? Or do you use both sides of your brain to do most things? Take the quiz at the link below to find out.

 Visit **www.emp.ca/ls** to learn more about your left and right brains.

Your Abilities

These are areas of life in which you feel strong and confident. Don't think of ability just as being smart in school. You could be smart with technology or body-smart—good at sports or dance.

Maybe you feel as though you were born with your abilities and can't change them. However, you can choose to develop your strengths and make them work for you. You can also improve areas where you feel less strong.

9-Smart

intelligence
the way a person understands

Years ago, a psychologist named Howard Gardner suggested that there were seven different kinds of **intelligence**, or seven different ways for people to be smart. Recently, two more intelligences were added. These nine intelligences are shown below. Most people are strong in two or more areas. For example, you might describe yourself as a "real people person" and also as someone who "thinks in words."

LEGEND
- You understand yourself well
- You think in words
- You see connections between ideas
- You think in pictures
- Your body is often in motion
- You think in sound and rhythm
- You understand other people well
- You relate to nature
- You love deep questions

How are you smart?

Jump In

1. a) In what ways are you smart? Study the pie graph on page 6. Which parts of the wheel seem to describe you best?

   b) Make a table like the one below in your notebook and fill it in. Under "Me," list some of the things you do that show you are smart this way. Review the intelligences wheel on page 6, along with the legend, for ideas. Check the ones that have the most examples. These are the main ways you are smart.

LM 1-4

Intelligence	Me	✓
Music Smart		
Body Smart		
People Smart		
Self Smart		
Picture Smart		
Word Smart		
Logic Smart		
Nature Smart		
Deep Smart		

   Place your completed chart in your portfolio.

2. Now that you know what your smarts are, are you surprised? Why or why not? Ask someone who knows you if he or she is surprised by your results.

3. Can you guess what types of intelligence your teacher has? What about your mother or father? How do you know?

4. Identify a time in school when your smarts have helped you. For example, you understood what a picture meant right away. Or you realized you knew how to build something by actually doing it.

5. With a partner, think of some jobs or types of work that would be good to do with your smarts. Do the same for your partner. Explain why you made these choices.

3-Style

People also learn in different ways. Some people like things written down. Some people are hands-on. Some people need to bounce ideas off someone else. These different ways of learning are called **learning styles**.

The three main styles are described in the chart below.

learning styles
three main ways to learn— through sight, hearing, or touch

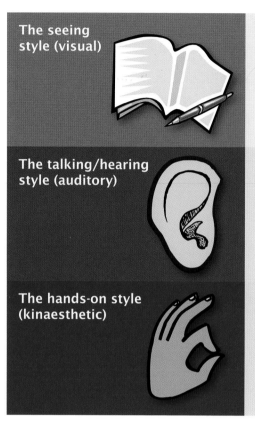

The seeing style (visual)	These people like to see it *on the page.* You might hear them saying, "I need to write that down or I'll forget it." They keep lots of notes and also like pictures and diagrams.
The talking/hearing style (auditory)	These people like things explained *through telling.* They also love to talk themselves! They would prefer to talk out an idea with someone than to study a paragraph in a book.
The hands-on style (kinaesthetic)	These people have to *do* something. They would rather jump in and try something than read the directions or look at a diagram. They may also use their hands a lot when they talk.

Jump In

1. a) What's your preferred learning style? Complete **Line Master 1-5: Seeing, Hearing, and Doing Quiz** to find out. This quiz takes about five minutes.

   b) How did you do? What is your preferred style? Are you surprised at the results? Why or why not?

Mix 'n' Match Styles

Many people prefer one learning style, but some people are a mix of two styles. For example, many talkers are also hands-on people.

You also might prefer one style depending on what you are doing. School is not always the ideal place for all learning styles!

Take advantage of homework time or special projects to unleash your own style. For example, if you're a hands-on learner, you could make a model of something you are studying in science. In English, you could ask to do a performance piece instead of a written report.

You can find more information on making the best of your learning style on **Line Master 1-6: Enhancing Your Learning Style.**

How to Listen—Even When It's Not Your Style

Listening seems to come more naturally to some people than to others. However, there are ways to improve your listening ability. Practise the following activities several times and watch your listening curve go up and up.

Listening Tips

1. "Did You Get That?"

In this game, your teacher or another student reads something out loud. It could be a set of directions, a want ad, an address, or something similar. Examples are found on **Line Master 1-7: Did You Get That?** Whoever reads will read this information aloud slowly, but only once. Write down what you heard, or take turns repeating what you heard. Try to remember as many specifics as possible. For example, try to remember "two years" in "Bike for sale, only two years old."

Leaning in toward the person who is speaking, and smiling, are two signals that you are really listening.

2. Listen and Paraphrase

Work with a partner to take turns reading some text aloud. You can choose from the articles in Part 2, which starts on page 30, or some other text you feel comfortable reading. Read only one paragraph at a time. Your partner must paraphrase what you have read. (Paraphrasing means stating the information in your own words.) Then, switch places with your partner.

3. Ask a Question

Some people just naturally tune out when listening. When you feel this way, try thinking of a question you would like to ask the speaker. Wait for a pause and then ask the speaker to clarify or go over what he or she has said. Chris Kaman, an NBA centre, uses this technique during huddles (see page 113).

4. Give Feedback

The next time a student presents in class, give that person feedback on his or her presentation. You can use **Line Master 1-8: Feedback Ideas**. Be respectful and specific in your advice. Being specific shows that you listened.

Practise the Skill

Pick one of the activities above and do it with a small group of students or with a partner. After you have done the activity several times, write down how you think it is improving your listening ability. How does listening better help you learn smart?

Place your statement in your portfolio.

Jump In

1. Think about your own learning in different subject areas during the past week. Record the following on **Line Master 1-9: My Learning Styles Profile**:

   a) the ways you like to learn (e.g., note-taking, drawing pictures)

   b) the challenges you face in learning (e.g., you tune out when listening)

   c) some new ways to learn that you will try (see **Line Master 1-6** for ideas)

   d) your least preferred learning situations and ideas for coping with them.

      Place your completed Learning Styles Profile in your portfolio.

2. You are asked to present information to the class on a topic you enjoy. What kind of presentation would you do? Choose one from the list below. In a few sentences, explain how your choice would suit your preferred learning style.

   a) You talk to the class with the help of some notes.

   b) You read your prepared notes to the class word for word.

   c) You use audio-visual tools such as a slide show or a DVD.

   d) You act out your presentation.

How to Create Motivation and Interest

This is so boring.
I'm never going to use this.
Just tell me how much it counts on the exam.

Do you recognize these statements? Every student has made them. Every teacher has heard them. Maybe you've even made them yourself!

During the last 50 years, research has revealed a lot about the human brain. Today we know that learning doesn't happen when you're bored. Learning happens when you're interested. That goes for you and for everybody else, including your friends, parents, and teachers.

When you're interested in something, you are motivated to learn. Without even thinking about it, you create the right conditions for learning:

- You remain open to learning more.
- You don't distract yourself.
- You see the point of it all.
- When you run across a difficult idea, you don't give up—you believe you can understand.

You may be thinking, "That's fine for when I'm interested. What about when I'm not interested?"

Well, there is no magic formula. However, there are some things you can do to create motivation. Once you do that, interest often follows.

Motivation Tips

1. Believe You Can Succeed

It turns out that what you believe about learning is key. If you believe you will fail at

a task, you will. Turn your beliefs around, and you may have a better chance at succeeding.

Even if you don't quite believe, act as if you do. Here's an experiment to try. Decide to smile for 30 seconds. Do you notice how your mood improves? That's because the act of smiling triggers hormones that make you feel good. Deciding to believe in yourself can have a similar effect.

2. See the Point of the Task

Most people are bored by learning that doesn't relate to them. With your teacher, make sure you understand why you are learning something. If you can't see the point of a task, try imagining the type of person who needs that information. How might you be like that person?

3. A Little Knowledge Helps

Think of your brain as the carpet side of a Velcro fastener. The hook needs just a bit of carpet to stick. Similarly, new knowledge needs to stick to something in your brain. That something is the knowledge you already have. (Tip: This book will give you lots of carpet!)

4. Say When You Don't Get It

Many students avoid speaking up when they don't understand. But saying you don't understand is *learning smart*. In business, it's always the smart guy who says, "I don't get it. Could you please clarify?" If you don't feel comfortable asking a question in front of your friends, arrange to see your teacher outside of class time.

5. Make It a Game

The human brain loves games. When you play a game, you usually forget about everything else. You enjoy the challenge, and you learn from your mistakes. Simple games for studying with a friend can be found in **Line Master 1-10: Games to Study By**. You can also ask your teacher to give you homework in the form of a game or problem.

6. Identify Your Curiosity

Nothing fires your brain like the personal urge to know more. What are you really, really interested in? How would you go about learning more about that topic? What can you learn from the way you learn when you are interested?

Sophie thinks she is not technology smart. However, she wants to use all the features of her new cell phone. How has she motivated herself? Try to find the six tips from pages 11–12 in the cartoon.

Practise the Skill

1. Imagine a time when you had a powerful learning experience. Perhaps you were at school, or maybe you were just hanging around with your friends. Maybe a coach tied a ribbon around one of your legs so that you could remember your pivot foot.

   a) How did you learn what was being taught?

   b) What learning style did you use? (See page 8 for learning styles.)

   c) What was your motivation for learning?

   d) Identify something you did that helped you learn in that situation that you could apply to a school situation.

This chapter introduced you to the following ideas:

- Knowing yourself—your interests, abilities, and preferred learning style—is the first step in learning how to learn smart.

- Your brain has a creative side and an analytic side. Most people feel they are more creative or more analytic.

- There are nine intelligences, or "smarts." Most people have more than one kind of smarts. You can have one kind of smarts or a combination.

- There are three main learning styles. These are described on page 8. Use your preferred style to learn smart.

- Listening is something everyone needs to do. You can improve your listening skills by using the strategies described on page 9.

- You can help to create interest and motivation even when you are bored or turned off. Find those tips on pages 11–12.

CHAPTER 2
The Manager of You Is You

Tara's Vanishing Day

How will Tara manage her day?

Where did this day go?

As her alarm went off at 7:30 a.m., Tara hit the five-minute snooze button and slid deeper under the covers. A few vague thoughts drifted into her mind about the day ahead. The Drama Club would meet after school today, and Tara definitely wanted to check it out. She also had to get going on her science project. That would mean library time.

Tara drifted off again. Not such a bad day.

At 8:15 a.m., Tara was frantically searching for clean jeans and her library card.

At 8:25, she was rushing to school (having forgotten her lunch) and talking by cell phone to her friend, Kevin.

"Hey, do you have time to go shopping with me for a soccer ball tonight?" Kevin asked.

"Sure," said Tara, hoping she wasn't late for school and completely forgetting about her earlier plans.

Later that night, as Tara wrapped up her third after-dinner call, she looked back on the day. Since she had forgotten her lunch, she'd been forced to buy a burger at the local mall (despite her recent vow to eat healthy). Since she hadn't found her library card, she couldn't take any science books out of the library. And since she blew her money for lunch, she had none left over for photocopying. "Hmm," she thought, "Science project: 1. Tara: 0."

Tara slapped her forehead. Only then did she remember that she had missed the Drama Club meeting in order to go shopping with Kevin. It was probably too late now to find out about this year's try-outs. And would she even have time? Seemed like she was always catching up instead of getting ahead.

Tara sighed. She was no further ahead with her **goals** than she had been yester-day, and she hadn't touched tonight's homework. Where *had* the time gone?

goals
things you want to achieve

Jump In

1. a) Tara had some things she wanted to do, but by day's end, she hadn't done any of them! Why not? Identify all the places where Tara's day fell off the radar and simply "vanished." Use a table like this one.

What Tara Did	How It Made the Day Vanish

   b) What "vanishing moments" have you experienced?

2. Now suggest some things that Tara could have done to keep her day on track.

3. If you were an employer, would you hire Tara after seeing her vanishing day caught on video? Explain your answer in a brief e-mail to Tara. Give at least two reasons.

What Do You Do All Day?

If you think that you have too many vanishing days, you are not alone. Most people admit they could use their time better.

When experts help people with time management, they start by asking them how they spend their time. Do you know how much time you actually spend on different activities each day? Maybe you think you spend a reasonable amount of time on homework, and much less time on television or talking with friends.

The key to managing your time is knowing

- what you want to do and
- how much time you need to spend on each activity to do it well.

Jump In

1. a) On day 1, try keeping a record of all your activities. Don't forget anything! Here is a list to get you started:

eating	clubs and sports	faith-related activities
sleeping	entertainment	volunteering
exercising	shopping	part-time work
going to class	chores	
studying and homework	family activities	

b) On day 2, put your list of activities in a table like this. You'll need lots of room in the second column. Keep this paper with you in a safe place, such as a three-ring binder or your jeans pocket.

My Activities	Time I Spent on This Activity	Time Totals
eating		

c) Every time you do this activity, write down how many minutes you spent on it. Separate your entries by "+" signs.

d) At the end of the day, add up all the minutes you spent on each activity. Remember to convert each 60 minutes to 1 hour. Example:

My Activities	Time I Spent on This Activity	Time Totals
eating	10 min + 25 min + 5 min + 40 min	80 min = 1 h, 20 min

e) Which activities soak up most of your time?

f) Which activities do you spend little time on?

g) Was there anything you missed doing today that you had planned to do?

h) What would you like to change about the amount of time you spend on certain activities? Place your activity log and your response to question (e) in your portfolio.

Making Time for Everything

Now that you know what you do all day, you can begin to shift some things around. Perhaps you want to devote more time to certain tasks, such as homework or hobbies that interest you.

To accomplish this, you will need to set some goals. You will also need an **agenda** to keep track of your time. Your agenda should have space to

- schedule activities
- write out your daily, weekly, and monthly goals.

agenda
a tool for organizing your time by day, week, month, and year

First, block off times for all the things you *must do*. These are your high-priority tasks. You can schedule other activities around these tasks. Don't forget the must-do's of eating and sleeping!

FEBRUARY

5 Monday

10:20 a.m. Careers report

3:30 p.m. Dentist appointment

6 Tuesday

4:00 p.m. Swim team tryouts

7 Wednesday

11:00 a.m. Math test, Unit 2

8 Thursday

3:30 p.m. Library date with Sarah for
English essay?

FEBRUARY

9 Friday

7:30 p.m. - 9:00 p.m. Roller-skating with
Liz and Marcus ☺

Dance marathon is Feb 15!

10 Saturday

9:00 a.m. Take Carey to Y

11 Sunday

● Weekly Goals

Tidy room
Bring back library books
Try out for swim team
Start English essay

Four-way agenda tips:

1. Must-Do: Block out your must-do activities in highlighter at the start of the week.

2. Write your weekly goals beside or below your weekly schedule.

3. Use your agenda to note assignment deadlines.

4. Use your agenda during announcements to note items of interest.

Now you can set some goals. It can be challenging to set goals if you have never done it before. That's okay; on page 19 you'll start small.

Getting Organized

Being organized makes it easier to be the manager of yourself. Remember Tara's frantic search for her jeans and library card on page 15? Rushing around looking for her stuff made Tara late. Being late put her under stress (a topic covered later in this chapter). And being under stress caused Tara to forget her most important goals of the day.

Guess what! Tara completely re-organized her room. Have a look at what she did.

What happened to...?

1	The library card	In her wallet, where it belongs
2	The jeans	In the dresser or in the laundry
3	The messy desk	Cleaned, with school supplies in easy reach
4	The knapsack	Emptied at night, next to the desk for packing tomorrow
5	The phone	Turned off!
6	The clock	Set 15 minutes earlier to avoid morning rush

What's new?

7	The desk lamp	To see what she is reading and writing
8	The script	To prepare for her small part in the school play
9	The file folders	To hold research and information on projects
10	The attitude	From stressed to calm and focused!

CHAPTER 2: THE MANAGER OF YOU IS YOU

Jump In

1. With a partner, think about a small personal goal for the rest of today. It might be something like attending all your classes today or making it to work on time. Next, think about personal goals and goals related to school. It might be helpful to review the list in activity 1 on page 16. With your partner, fill in a table like the one below.

My Goals	School	Personal
A goal for today		
A goal for tomorrow		
A goal for this week		
A goal for this month		

LM 2-3

2. Now, transfer your goals into your agenda. If you must achieve your goal by a certain time, write down the time, for example: "Get to the Y by 4 p.m." If your goal is something you intend to do but don't need to schedule, simply write it down as your weekly or monthly goal. At the end of the week or month, cross it out if you achieved it.

3. Announcing the "Extreme Bedroom Makeover"! How could you change your own room to make it more organized for studying and for after-school activities?

   a) Take some "before" photos of your room and study them.

   b) Make a list of the things you should change. Try to identify three.

   c) Make over your room and snap your "after" photos.

   d) Bring both sets of photos to class mounted on paper. Label all the "don'ts" on your before photos and all the "do's" on your after photos.

   e) Be able to summarize the changes you made and the reasons for the changes.

4. Alternative: The "Extreme Locker Makeover." Follow the same steps to make over your messy locker.

How to Homework without Sweating

Here are some simple rules for effective studying:

1. Know what you are supposed to be studying.
2. Have a plan of attack.
3. Have the space and the tools to study.
4. Know yourself.

Study Tips

1. Know What You Are Supposed to Be Studying

It starts in class, when you get an assignment. Make sure you write down all assignments, including homework, and the dates they are due. The best place to put all the information is your agenda (see page 17). If you don't understand an assignment, ask your teacher to clarify it.

2. Have a Plan of Attack

What's your purpose? Are you researching an essay or studying for a test? You should plan your studying accordingly.

For all assignments:

- Read the directions for the assignment a few times. Make sure you understand what you are supposed to do. If your teacher is not available, ask another student for help.

For regular homework:

- Break up tasks into small chunks.
- Think about how long each task will take you and spread them out. Skim the material. It might be a problem to solve or text you must read. To skim, look at everything quickly first. Do not be put off by parts you don't understand. Keep skimming to find parts you do understand. Begin there and work outward.

Making a model of an idea sometimes lets you see how it really works.

- If you are reading, pay close attention to the top and bottom of the text. Important ideas often come "early" and "late."

For essays:

- Use **Line Master 7-8: Essay Planning Templates**. It will guide you in the entire process.
- Look at the tasks involved, break them into chunks, and spread them out over several weeks.
- Keep a file folder with the essay name on it at home. Place all the material related to the essay in that file.
- Take out the file and review it every couple of days, even if you are not planning to work on your essay that day.

3. Have the Space and the Tools to Study

Know what books and materials you need to study. Decide which materials can stay at home and organize them in one spot. Make sure you have enough light! If you don't think you have suitable space at home to study, talk to your teacher or guidance counsellor. Together, you can explore some alternatives to studying at home.

4. Know Yourself

Respect your personal learning style when you study! (For more on learning styles, see Chapter 1, pages 8–9.) Here are some tips.

For the "seeing" style:

- Look at the pictures first. Check out any diagrams or maps in the book.
- Use a graphic organizer if your teacher has provided one.
- Make your own organizer or mind map to display information (see Skills Workshop, page 54).

For the "talking/hearing" style:

- Try reading your material out loud.
- Study with a buddy. Paraphrase what you are reading, or explain an idea out loud to your buddy. (For more on paraphrasing, see Skills Workshop, page 9.)

For the "hands-on" style:

- Take frequent breaks and walk around.
- With a buddy, role-play what you are studying, such as the events in a novel.
- Try to make a physical model of concepts you are studying in math or science.

Practise the Skill

1. a) Identify an assignment you are working on now.
   b) From the information above, identify at least two strategies that you could use to improve the way you are handling that assignment. Try these new strategies sometime soon.
   d) Write down how using the new strategies made studying easier.

The Five-Day Countdown: Test Preparation Plan

This is a great plan for studying for a test. You need to commit five days. Every day gets you more ready. Here's how to do it:

- **Day 5.** Read over your textbook and class notes. Go back over your notes a second time and try to pick out one key piece of information from each page. Highlight it, mark it with a sticky note, or find some other way of making that information important. If you have a test outline from your teacher, check back over the notes you made and try to connect them to the outline.

- **Day 4.** Use your favourite learning strategies to help you remember the information you identified on day 5. (See activity 1b) on page 7.)

- **Day 3.** Rewrite the information, using as few words as possible. Use abbreviations or symbols such as ON for Ontario (abbreviation) or ♀ for population (symbol).

- **Day 2.** Write out the questions that are going to be on the test. Then answer each one.

- **Day 1.** This is the day you take your test. Review your written notes from day 3. Review the questions and answers you prepared on day 2. You can do this while eating breakfast, walking on the treadmill—it's up to you. Just before the test, go over any information you are having difficulty remembering.

Practise the Skill

Think about what you should do each day of the five-day test preparation plan. For each day, write a sentence that tells you what you will do that day.

Day 5	
Day 4	
Day 3	
Day 2	
Day 1	

Time Blasters

Despite your best intentions, you may still have problems managing yourself and your time. Everyone does. This next section examines some common challenges.

Procrastinating

Procrastinating means putting off a task you should do. "I'll do it later," you say. "I've got lots of time."

Why do people procrastinate? The reasons are many. Here are some common ones, and ways to avoid being a procrastinator.

"It's too hard." Actually, the hardest part is starting something. Next time you have an assignment, try starting it. Commit no more than five or 10 minutes to it. Once you have started a task, you will find it easier to return to it.

"It's too big." Does the task look huge? You can address this problem by taking your agenda and breaking up the task into smaller chunks.

"It's confusing." Remember, it's the smart guy who admits he's confused. Ahead of time, it's important to clarify the task or the material with your teacher. After school, it's OK to ask another student for help.

"I'm going to fail." Worrying will not make the task go away. Remember that what you believe about a task is important (see Skills Workshop, page 11, tip 1). Go back over those tips and see if one of them can help you crack the task.

"I've got better things to do." Review your goals (page 19). Do you really have better things to do, or are you just avoiding something?

Worrying about failure is one cause of procrastination.

procrastinating
avoiding a task
by putting it off
until later

Jump In

1. Are you a procrastinator? Use **Line Master 2-4: Are You a Procrastinator?** to find out.

2. With a partner, identify the situations that make you procrastinate the most. Write down the two most challenging ones. Beside each situation, write down something that you could do to avoid procrastination. Review the tips above for ideas.

Insisting on Perfection

Perfectionism sometimes goes with procrastination. When you are a perfectionist, you are afraid to do anything that is less than perfect. As a result, you may turn in assignments late because you fear they are not your best. Or you may spend too much time perfecting a little detail and not enough time on the big picture.

One way to deal with perfectionism is to talk to your teacher. He or she can help you see that your job at school is not about being perfect; it's about learning—and that means making mistakes.

Another tip is to change your self-talk. Perfectionists sometimes engage in negative self-talk. It sounds like this: "I'm so stupid." "I've got to do much better than that." Try to stop yourself every time you engage in negative self-talk. Try using a special word that cues you to stop (e.g., NOT, stop, see ya). Then see if you can replace those statements with positive statements:

- "People are allowed to make mistakes."
- "Hey, I did better than last time."
- "I blew one part but I got a lot right."

Jump In

1. Create some positive self-talk to replace this negative self-talk:

   a) "I'll never be good enough."

   b) "I can't hand this in—it looks like garbage."

   c) "Another one of my stupid mistakes and I quit."

   d) "This will never look the way I want it to."

   e) "Other people can do it, so why can't I?"

2. Design a bracelet with a slogan on it that puts perfectionism in its place. Use words and symbols. Be firm, but don't be rude! Example: "Why be perfect when I can be me?"

Giving Up Too Soon

Giving up before you're done is another big time waster. If you start a task and fail to complete it, what happens? You often have to go back to it anyway. You forget your train of thought. You lose time! Try these tips to help you persevere with tasks:

- Reward yourself for finishing tasks, even small ones. Tell yourself how great you are for getting it done.
- Work with a buddy. It takes more energy to cancel a study date than to get the task done.
- When you need to finish something, avoid people who want to get you off-task.
- Have a realistic schedule for completing tasks. Go back to your agenda (page 17) or homework plan (pages 20–21).
- Think about the real consequences of not finishing what you are doing. What are they?

Jump In

1. With a partner, role-play staying on-task while your partner tempts you to quit. Then, reverse roles.

   a) What strategies did you use to avoid quitting?

   b) What strategies did your partner use to avoid quitting?

2. Which strategy do you predict will work best for you the next time you want to give up? Write down your no-quit strategy and why it works for you. Place that information in your portfolio.

Your study buddy can keep you on track when you feel like giving up.

Staying Well

It's easier to learn—and to manage yourself—when you feel well. You can get a head start on wellness by eating right, exercising regularly, and getting enough sleep.

Choosing the Right Diet

Your diet is important because many nutrients help your brain work better. Canada's Food Guide recommends that teenagers eat a variety of foods, including several servings from each food group: cereals and grains, fruits and vegetables, dairy products, and protein. Eating some of these foods every day will help you operate at peak performance.

Food Guide Basics
- Choosing Foods
- Using the Food Guide
- Maintaining Healthy Habits

Canada's Food Guide to Healthy Eating	
Nutrition Do's	**Nutrition Don'ts**
• Eating a variety of food groups	• Dieting
• Eating breakfast	• Skipping meals
• Drinking water and low-fat milk instead of pop	• Eating too much sugar and caffeine
• Limiting your fast-food habit	• Eliminating a whole food group without asking your doctor

Visit **www.emp.ca/ls** to examine Canada's Food Guide in more detail and take the guided tour.

Exercise and Your Brain

Regular exercise can help your brain! How does it work?

Just moving around delivers more oxygen to your brain, which makes your brain work better. But it gets more interesting than that. Scientists have been able to show that regular exercise can improve a person's memory, ability to concentrate, and ability to plan and organize.

The ideal amount of exercise for most people is 30-60 minutes a day at least three times a week. Exercise should raise your heart rate to its **training range** in order to keep your heart healthy.

training range
65–75 percent of your maximum heart rate based on your age

Jump In

1. Take an inventory of your own nutrition and exercise habits and compare them with the guidelines found on page 26. Examine Canada's Food Guide, the Nutrition Do's and Don'ts, and exercise recommendations. How are you shaping up?

2. Select one way to improve your physical health over the next week. At the end of the week, write down what you did and what kind of success you had.

When Stress Gets You Down

Stress is a force pushing against you. It can push you from the inside or from the outside. A little stress is good—it makes you feel alive! However, too much stress is bad for you and can certainly affect your learning.

Examples of inside stress include the decisions you make (e.g., putting off a task instead of starting it) or your personality (e.g., expecting too much of yourself). You have already examined several ways to approach these kinds of stresses.

The other kind of stress is outside you. It comes from events that you have less control over. This stress is called external stress.

How can you deal with events you can't control? In fact, many of the things you are already trying to do will help you with stress. Exercise is a proven stress-buster. So is spending time doing your favourite thing. Listening to music, watching television, or just talking to a friend can also relieve stress in the short term.

What about external stresses that are also unlawful or against school policy, such as racism or bullying? You may need to report the incident to a school administrator. In *Learn Smart*, especially in Chapter 9, you will find lots of ideas on how to stand up for yourself and take appropriate action in situations like that.

stress
forces acting on the body from the inside or the outside

Top External Stressors for Teens

- Death of a parent
- Parent's new relationship
- Parents' divorce
- Separation
- Birth or adoption of new sibling
- Fighting with parents
- Academic pressure
- Being bullied
- Lack of friends
- Moving

Being bullied is a major source of stress for teens and children.

PART 2
Practise Your Skills

In this section of *Learn Smart*, you will have the opportunity to

- use a wide variety of reading strategies
- read and understand different texts and visual information
- ask questions, problem-solve, clarify your thinking, and present ideas
- create different texts and graphics for different purposes and audiences
- use math procedures and concepts in real-life tasks
- connect problem-solving in math to other areas of life
- use teamwork and interpersonal skills in a variety of situations
- identify the benefits of teamwork
- identify actions, characteristics, skills, and resources that enhance learning and growth

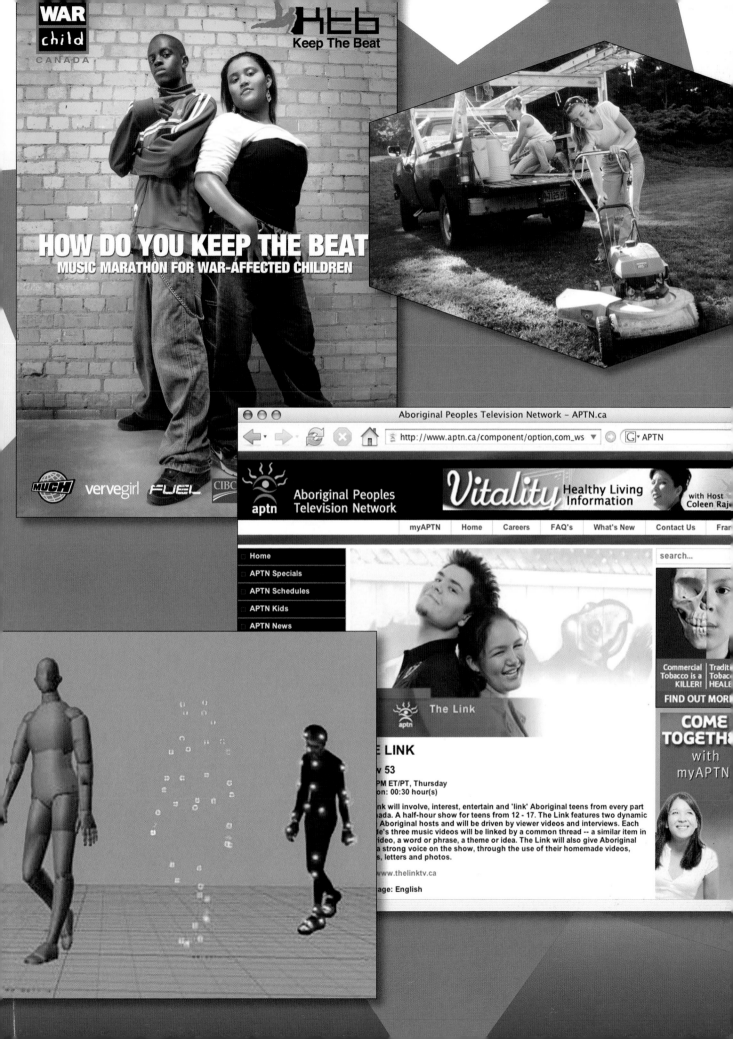

CHAPTER 3
Out There

Storm Chaser!

Connect the Text
- What experiences have you had with storms and bad weather?
- What weather events are now in the news?

Reading Strategy

As you read this article, highlight or underline the key words and phrases, not whole sentences, that describe people who chase storms and their reasons for chasing them.

Storm chasers are people with a passion for violent weather. They chase **tornadoes**, **hurricanes**, and other severe storms and photograph them for fun or for scientific research. Some storm chasers are also "spotters" who report storms to local weather authorities.

tornadoes
strong windstorms with funnel clouds

hurricanes
bad storms with a wind speed of at least 119 km/h

1

Chasers track a supercell thunderstorm. Supercell storms have deep, rotating updrafts (rising air). Can you spot the rotation in this supercell?

Record-size hail!

As hobbies go, storm chasing is not for the timid. Lightning, flooding, **hail**, high winds, and flying objects—from frogs to refrigerators—are all in a day's work. Canadian storm chaser George Kourounis once got so close to a tornado in Oklahoma City that his car was actually inside it! He didn't waste any time photographing the swirling **debris** around his windshield.

2

hail
lumps of ice that form in a storm cloud and drop to the ground

Storm chasing does have its quiet moments. It has been said that 95 percent of the time, storm chasing means "driving under blue skies while getting into position, trying to figure out where the storms will form."

3

debris
what is left over after something has been broken up

Storm chasing is not an inexpensive hobby. Storm chasers often drive for long distances to reach active storms. Some install detection equipment in their cars to help them spot weather in the distance. Because they're usually not **meteorologists**, storm chasers spend time and money learning how to forecast weather and track storms in motion.

4

meteorologists
people who study and forecast the weather

Interested in chasing your own storms? The pros say, learn all you can about weather and maintain an attitude of "doing it safely." Check out the link below to learn more about storm chasing.

5

Visit **www.emp.ca/ls** to access links to storm-chasing Web sites, message boards, and blogs.

Read for Meaning

1. Refer to your highlighted or underlined words and phrases. Write two to three sentences in your own words describing storm chasers and their reasons for storm chasing.
2. Describe at least two dangers of storm chasing mentioned in the article.
3. Which phrase or sentence tells how storm chasers perform a service to communities?

☑☐

Sharpen Your Writer's Craft

1. In the first sentence of the article, suggest another word for "violent."
2. Explain why the word "spotters," in paragraph 1, is in quotation marks.
3. Why does paragraph 5 begin with an incomplete sentence? With a question?
4. How does the picture of the hailstones support the information that you read in the text?

☑☐

Jump In

1. You have a $2000 budget to outfit your car with the latest storm-chasing technology. Go shopping using **Line Master 3-1: The Storm Chaser's Store**. There you will find
   - 15 different gadgets
   - a brief description and price of each item.

   Your task is to select the very best technology and keep within your budget. You must also give a reason why you selected each item. Your reason should be written as a complete sentence and be related to storm chasing. Watch out! Not all the items are equally useful. Use **Line Master 3-2: Storm Chaser Purchases** to help you keep track of your reasons and your spending.

2. Hurricanes have category numbers to describe how severe they are. Read the following table and answer the questions.

Category	Wind Speed (km/hour)	Signs of Damage
1	119–153	• Signs and tree branches knocked down • Small plants destroyed • Loose objects blown away
2	154–177	• Mobile homes damaged • Some roofs, doors, windows of buildings damaged
3	178–209	• Whole trees blown down • Many mobile homes destroyed • Some roads flooded
4	210–249	• Roofs blown off most buildings • Collapsed lower floors in many buildings • Complete destruction of mobile homes
5	> 249	• Complete roof failure in most buildings • Total collapse of many buildings

a) Which category number describes the most severe storm?

b) Based on these wind speeds, what is the corresponding hurricane category?
   i) 162 km/h   ii) 278 km/h   iii) 125 km/h   iv) 203 km/h

c) You live in a two-storey building and a Category 4 storm is about to hit your community.
   - Where should you *not* go to be safe? Why?
   - Where do you think you should go?

3. Examine the objects below. In the following activity, you will find the diameter of each. The diameter of an object is an imaginary line that passes right through its centre. The length of that line, from edge to edge, equals the object's diameter.

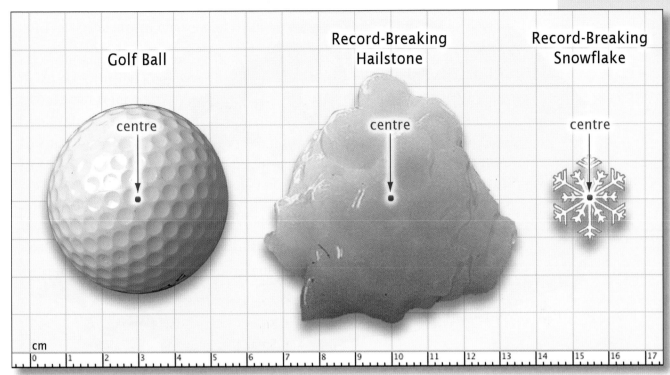

Objects are shown at their actual size.

To find the largest diameter of each object, put the edge of your ruler through the centre of each one. You may have to turn your ruler around to do this. Remember, the largest diameter will be where there is the greatest distance from edge to edge.

a) What is the diameter of the golf ball?

b) What is the largest diameter of the large hailstone?

c) What is the largest diameter of the large snowflake?

d) The diameter of an average hailstone is 1.75 cm. How many times larger than an average hailstone is this hailstone?

e) The diameter of an average snowflake is 0.65 cm. How many times larger than an average snowflake is this snowflake?

4. Create a written or video news report or storyboard of the life of a storm— before, during, and after. Your presentation should answer the following questions:

- What kind of storm was it?
- What caused the storm?
- How did people know the storm was coming?
- What did people say about the storm? (Make up some quotations.)
- What happened during the storm?
- What damage did the storm cause?

Use **Line Master 3-4: Elements of a News Story** to guide you.

Be Your Own Counterfeit Detective

Connect the Text

■ Have you ever been "stuck" with a counterfeit bill? What did you do?

Reading Strategy

1. Read the title of the text. What do you think this article is about?
2. Study the images. What do you think is happening in the pictures? Explain why.

ultraviolet
on the light spectrum, so violet that humans cannot see it

counterfeit
imitation meant to pass as real; fake

Saahir withdrew $60 from a bank machine after working a part-time shift at the supermarket. Next day, he tried to buy a notebook with one of the $20 bills. The cashier looked at the bill. She touched it, tilted it, and ran it under an **ultraviolet** (UV) light. She frowned at Saahir and called over the store manager: the $20 was **counterfeit**. 1

Saahir couldn't believe it. The money came from the bank! How could it be fake? Fortunately, the store manager believed him. By law, however, he could not give Saahir back the counterfeit bill. He had to turn it over to the RCMP. 2

Saahir is out $20. He's not too happy about it. 3

WISE WORDS

"The bank doesn't reimburse consumers for counterfeit money."
— *Lisa Elliot, Bank of Canada*

What is Saahir about to discover?

Checking for Fakes

Saahir went online. He learned how the RCMP and the Bank of Canada have teamed up to educate the public and fight counterfeiting. Suspect a bill? Then check it. You should be able to answer "yes" to all the following questions.

4

1. **Touch** Does the bill feel like other bills?

2. **Tilt** Do the special maple leaves or colour patches change colour?

3. **Look at** Are fine printing and **microprinting** sharp? Does a UV light reveal fluorescent fibres?

4. **Look through** Are watermarks and woven security threads (in new **currency**) visible?

microprinting printing technique that uses tiny print

A Canadian $10 bill is magnified by a powerful microscope in an RCMP lab.

Saahir also discovered how counterfeiters use computer technology to make new and better fakes. In response, the Bank of Canada keeps adding new security features to Canada's currency. Check out the link below to find out more about counterfeiting.

5

currency money that is in circulation today

Visit **www.emp.ca/ls** to read more news and information about protecting yourself from counterfeit money.

Read for Meaning

1. What is the purpose of this article?
2. Why was Saahir surprised to learn that one of the bills was fake?
3. Why did the cashier not simply return the fake $20 note to him?
4. Rephrase this sentence so that it will have the same meaning: "Saahir is out $20."
5. What does the acronym "RCMP" stand for? How is this acronym made up?
6. Read the steps for checking any currency that seems suspicious. Make up an acronym that will help you remember the steps.

Sharpen Your Writer's Craft

1. Find words from the article that mean the same as the following:
   a) money   b) characteristics   c) miniature text   d) show
2. Provide words that mean the opposite of the following:
   a) visible   b) micro

Jump In

1. The store manager has taken away Saahir's $20 bill. Now he is upset. He wants his money back, but by law the manager must keep it. Saahir can respond in three different ways: aggressively, passively, or assertively. These three ways are shown below.

Type of Communication		What You Do
Aggressive communication		• Raise your voice • Blame • Call names • Force or threaten
Passive communication		• Speak quietly • Don't say what you need or how you feel • Feel angry inside
Assertive communication		• Speak confidently • Ask for what you want politely • Show that you understand how the other person feels

a) Write what Saahir would say and do if he spoke to the store manager using
   - aggressive communication
   - passive communication
   - assertive communication.

b) Which type of communication do you think will work best to help Saahir get what he wants? Why?

c) A cashier gives you a $10 bill in change. When you touch the bill it feels too smooth, and when you tilt it the colour does not change. You are fairly sure it is counterfeit. Write what you would say to the cashier using assertive communication.

2. Put yourself in Saahir's place. You have used assertive communication successfully. The store manager has agreed to help you. He suggests that you write a letter of complaint to the bank manager explaining what happened at their bank machine. He tells you to
   - write it in a formal letter style
   - say clearly what happened
   - ask for something to be done to correct the problem.

   Use **Line Master 3-6: How to Write a Formal Letter** to guide you.

3. Phew! Saahir has checked all the other bills in his wallet, and none of them is counterfeit. Here is what he finds in his wallet:

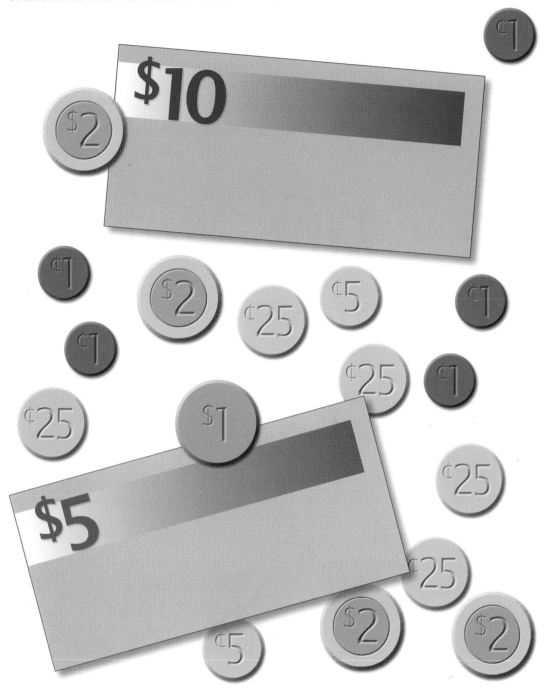

a) How much money does Saahir have in his wallet?

b) Saahir spends $2.52 at a convenience store. How many of each bill and coin will he need to pay his bill exactly without any change?

c) Saahir likes to have as few coins in his wallet as possible. How should he pay for his $14.66 bill at the grocery store to get the fewest coins back as change?

i)	1 × $10	1 × $5	1 × 5¢	1 × 1¢
ii)	1 × $10	2 × $2	3 × 25¢	1 × 1¢
iii)	1 × $10	1 × $5		

Empower Yourself

Self-Advocacy

1. Counterfeiters make fake money. In a sense, they are cheating the public (like Saahir) out of their money.

   a) As a class, discuss what would motivate someone to make counterfeit money. List your reasons on a chalkboard or a piece of chart paper.

   b) Have you ever been aware of students cheating at school? As a class, generate another list of all the reasons that could motivate students to cheat at school.

   c) In a group of two to five students, look at the two lists of reasons people cheat. Decide which of the reasons are understandable and which ones are never defensible. Use a T-chart to separate the reasons. An example has been done for you.

Reasons We Understand	Reasons That Are Never Acceptable
They want to please their parents.	They made a bet that they could get away with it.

   d) Saahir feels he was treated unfairly when the store manager took away his $20 bill. Sometimes students feel they have been treated unfairly at school. Working in your group, generate a list of all the things you feel are unfair at school.

   e) Each group should take a turn reporting its ideas to the rest of the class. As each group reports, the other groups should add ideas to their lists.

   f) In your group, rank the unfair school practices, with 1 being the most unfair. Share your rankings with the class. Together, create a list of the top three unfair practices that take place at school.

   g) In your group, use **Line Master 3-7: Injustice Organizer** to determine what could be done about the unfair practices that exist at school.

Problem	Responsibility	Resources Needed	Solution Looks Like

   Consider the following questions:

   • What is the unfair practice?

   • Who is responsible for fixing the problem?

   • What resources (time, money, outside support) are needed to fix the problem?

   • What does the solution look like at school? How would you know the problem was fixed?

h) In your group, complete **Line Master 3-8: The Three-Step Interview**. During this process, one person will play a student advocate and one person will play the principal. The other students will take notes.

Remember: The student is trying to convince the principal to take action against one of the examples of injustice at school. The students who are taking notes should record the best arguments the student makes that convince the principal to take action.

Repeat the process so that each student has the chance to role-play all roles. When your group is finished, you should have one piece of paper containing all recorders' notes.

LM 3-9

i) In your group, create an invitation asking the principal or another member of the school leadership team to visit your class and listen to your concerns.

j) On your own, prepare point-form notes about one of the issues of injustice facing the school. These notes will form the basis of your presentation to the principal. Share your notes with other members of your group and get suggestions.

k) Practise your presentations to the principal in small groups or in front of the class. Ask other students to offer constructive criticism:

- Are your points convincing? For more on being convincing, see the Skills Workshops How to Make a Good Argument, page 115, and How to Be Persuasive, page 147.
- Will your presentation achieve the desired result?

Practising first always lets you improve your presentation through feedback.

Jump In

1. Study the table showing the results of doping tests at the Summer Olympic Games.

Year	Location	Number of Tests	Number of Violations
1968	Mexico City	667	1
1972	Munich	2079	7
1976	Montreal	786	11
1980	Moscow	645	0
1984	Los Angeles	1507	12
1988	Seoul	1598	10
1992	Barcelona	1848	5
1996	Atlanta	1923	2
2000	Sydney	2359	11
2004	Athens	3667	26*

* Includes positive doping tests as well as other violations of the anti-doping rules, such as not arriving on time for a test.

Source: International Olympic Committee

a) Which Olympic Games had the lowest number of tests as well as the lowest number of violations? State the year and the location.

b) Which Olympic Games had the highest number of tests and violations?

c) Find the percentage of athletes doping at each of the Olympic Games. (Divide the number of violations by the number of tests, and multiply by 100.)

d) Which Olympic Games had the highest percentage of doping?

e) Why is there an asterisk (*) beside the number 26 in the last line of the table?

f) Why do you think there were an unusually high number of violations in Athens?

2. Caffeine is a legal drug found in many drinks. While it can give you pep, its side effects can be harmful. Study the amounts of caffeine in each of these items.

| (237 mL) | (355 mL) | (355 mL) | (250 mL) | (43-g bar) |
| 135 mg | 26 mg | 40 mg | 80 mg | 30 mg |

Health Canada recommends that adults consume no more than 450 mg of caffeine a day.

a) Compare the cup of coffee and the bottle of iced tea. Which of these two beverages has a stronger dose of caffeine?

b) How much caffeine is found in two energy drinks? Is this amount more than the recommended limit?

c) A teacher has a cup of coffee on his drive to school, a second cup of coffee after his morning class, and a can of cola at lunch. How many chocolate bars can he eat before he reaches his daily caffeine maximum?

d) Think about the caffeine-containing foods and drinks that you consume. Estimate how much caffeine you consume in a day.

Visit www.emp.ca/ls to read more news and information about the caffeine content of different drinks and the dangers of abusing energy drinks.

3. Teen athletes are often pressured to play well for their school team. It is much easier to refuse banned drugs when you are prepared. Here are some ways to say "no" to drugs in the locker room, or at a party.

Your track and field practice is over. A teammate comes up to you with some pills, saying, "Take these, they'll give you the edge." Your job is to say no. Write a short script of this conversation using these refusal skills and **Line Master 3-10: Saying No Dramas.** When you are finished, act out your script with a partner.

Empower Yourself

Goal Setting

WISE WORDS

"When you take on a goal and put your heart and soul into doing everything it takes to accomplish that goal, that is excellence."

— *Olympic gold medalist Beckie Scott*

1. Study Beckie Scott's photo and read her Wise Words. With a partner, discuss the following questions. (Refer back to the text on page 45 if you need to.)
   a) What was Beckie's goal?
   b) What happened that prevented her from reaching her goal?
   c) How did these events probably make Beckie want her goal even more?
   d) How did Beckie get justice?

2. a) In a group of two to five students, consider the following questions and record your work on **Line Master 3-11: Activities and Goals Organizer**.
   i)   What are some of the activities that you feel passionate about? (Examples might include sports, music, hobbies, or a part-time job.)
   ii) What are some things that you would like to be excellent at?
   iii) How do people set goals for themselves?
   iv) Is it okay not to know what your goals are when you are a teenager?

   b) Share your organizer with the class. You can share your work orally or post the organizers so that every student has the chance to walk around and view them.

3. a) Share your goals with your partner and reflect on the things that will help you achieve your goals (enablers) and the things that will stand in your way (obstacles). Fill out the T-chart below with your ideas and your partner's ideas.

Enablers (things that help me reach my goals)	Obstacles (things that stand in my way)
Setting my alarm clock	Watching too much TV

b) As a class, discuss the following questions:
   i) If you could get rid of all the obstacles in your life, would you be able to achieve all of your goals?
   ii) What is the biggest obstacle to being successful in school?
   iii) What assistance do you need to overcome that obstacle—from others, and from yourself?

c) Create and complete the following chart in your notebook and keep it as part of your portfolio.

LM 3-12

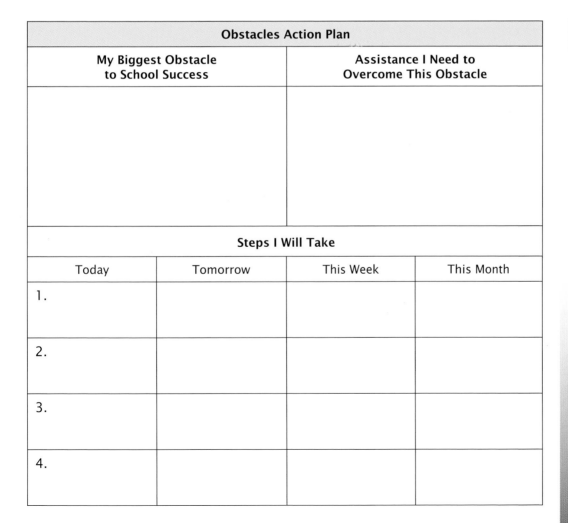

Obstacles Action Plan			
My Biggest Obstacle to School Success		Assistance I Need to Overcome This Obstacle	
Steps I Will Take			
Today	Tomorrow	This Week	This Month
1.			
2.			
3.			
4.			

Cha-Ching: Growing a Business from Your Passion

Connect the Text

- What is your passion? How do you know it's a passion?
- Have you had ideas for a business venture?

Reading Strategy

Create a mind map in your notebook. In the centre, write the word "business." Add as many words as you can that relate to starting a new business, for example, "staff."

Did you know that most teens have a secret dream? It's to start and run their own business. That's hardly surprising. After all, how many people really want to work for a boss?

1

But how can a student turn a dream of being an **entrepreneur** into reality? Some students do. And those who succeed offer one piece of advice: find your passion. That hobby that turns into a burning idea for a product or service and keeps you awake at night? Let it inspire you into action. And don't be afraid to talk about it—especially with people who have business **savvy**.

2

entrepreneur
a person who starts his or her own business

savvy
practical knowledge; hands-on know-how

WISE WORDS

"Sure, I run into people all the time who clearly have no confidence in me .... But I also count on the support of many more people who really believe in what I'm doing."

— Brad Leblanc, 17, talent agent

A passion for gardening = profit!

Billy Jack Grieves—
entrepreneur since age 18

Ben Cathers had a passion. He loved the Internet
and he loved advertising. Soon, Ben couldn't stop
thinking about how the Internet was the perfect
way to advertise goods and services. So he started
a business, at age 12, showing teens how to market
their services on the Internet. Seven years later,
his company employs 10 people, and Cathers has
become a business **guru**—for teen entrepreneurs.

3

guru
an expert guide;
someone who
knows a lot
about a particular
subject

Cathers says passion won't be enough. To succeed,
you will also need a business plan and market
research. "Most of the research is available online
for free," says Cathers. "Most of what you need is
available for free or at a very, very low cost, and if
you put the effort into it and you search around,
you'll definitely be able to find it."

4

What about balancing school, home, and business demands? Here the art of
negotiating can pay big **dividends**. Cathers got co-op credits for setting up and
running his company. Check out the link below to find out more about how you
can turn your passion into dollars.

5

dividends
rewards or
benefits resulting
from efforts

Visit **www.emp.ca/ls** for information about
business plans and Web sites just for teen entrepreneurs.

Read for Meaning

1. In your own words, summarize the approach suggested in paragraph 2 for
   developing a successful enterprise.
2. Many people do not know how to turn their passion into a business. What
   suggestions does Ben Cathers offer?
3. What is "the art of negotiating" as it is described in this article?
4. Why is Ben Cathers referred to as a "guru—for teen entrepreneurs"?
5. Who is the intended audience for this article? Explain your answer.

Sharpen Your Writer's Craft

1. Three of the article's paragraphs begin with a question. What is the effect on
   the reader?
2. The third sentence in paragraph 2 uses
   a colon (:). What purpose does it serve?
3. Two sentences in the article include a dash (—).
   Locate each dash and explain its purpose.
4. Use dot-jots to state the topic of each
   paragraph. Example:

Para 1 • introduces idea of running own business

Jump In

1. Charlie's Catering offers nutritious hot meals for up to 75 people. Recently, Charlie catered a youth conference held at a nearby community centre. Examine **Line Master 3-13: Charlie's Catering Spreadsheet** and answer the following questions:

    a) How many meals were served at the youth conference?

    b) Calculate the total sales from the event.

    c) After the expenses are paid for, how much did Charlie make?

    d) Charlie employs his friend Karl to help him prepare the food and to sell it at the event. He pays Karl $11 per hour. If Karl helped Charlie for five hours, how much profit did Charlie's business make from the event?

    e) What could Charlie do to reduce his expenses?

2. Rosalie goes to yard sales in her neighbourhood. She later sells her treasures online, shipping them to customers using a courier company.

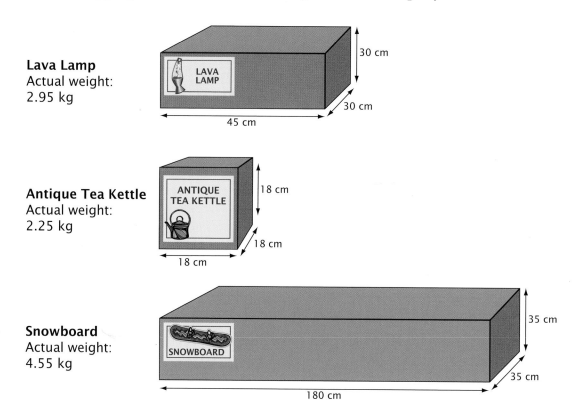

Lava Lamp
Actual weight: 2.95 kg

LAVA LAMP — 30 cm, 30 cm, 45 cm

Antique Tea Kettle
Actual weight: 2.25 kg

ANTIQUE TEA KETTLE — 18 cm, 18 cm, 18 cm

Snowboard
Actual weight: 4.55 kg

SNOWBOARD — 35 cm, 35 cm, 180 cm

   a) Which package is the heaviest?

   b) To find out how much the shipping will cost, Rosalie needs to calculate the **dimensional weight** of each package. For each package, multiply length (L) × width (W) × height (H), and then divide by 6000. (Dimensional weight is important to companies that ship packages for a fee. Even if a package doesn't weigh much, it may take up a lot of room in a plane or truck. That means it should cost more to ship that package.)

   c) If the actual weight is greater than the dimensional weight, the package costs more to ship. Which package will have an extra charge?

dimensional weight

$$\frac{L \times W \times H}{6000}$$

3. Business gurus tell teen entrepreneurs to find their passion. What is your passion, and how could you put that passion into a business?

   a) Create a mind map of your own skills and interests. (See the example below and the Skills Workshop on page 54.)

   b) Make a second mind map of products and services people use in your community.

   c) Write a sentence stating what type of business you would like to start.

   d) In several sentences, explain how you could use your skills and interests—your passion—to provide this product or service to your community.

KIYA'S MIND MAPS

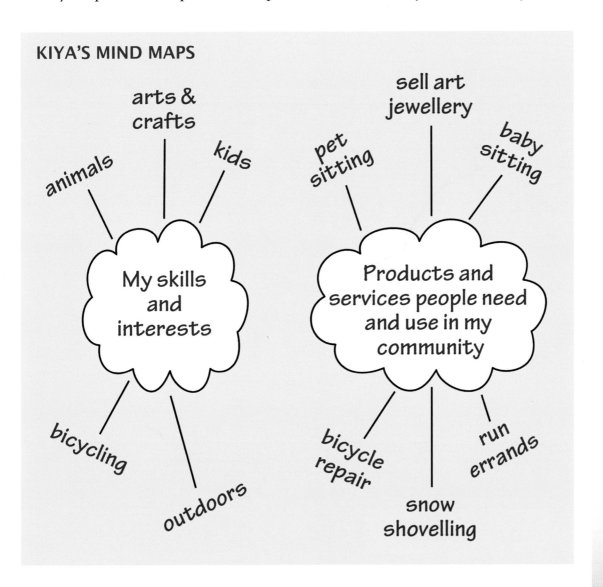

4. Write a plan for a business that you would like to start in your community. Your ideas from the previous activity should guide you. Use **Line Master 3-14: Writing a Business Plan** to help you get your business going.

How to Use Mind Maps

Mind maps are a visual way of recording information. They let you see the relationships between ideas instantly. Next to a mind map, a paragraph can look like a wall of text.

A mind map can easily display

- items in a list
- sections and subsections
- an idea or opinion, with evidence
- categories (hockey is in the category *sports*)
- steps in a process
- options (pizza or wings?)
- pros and cons.

And much, much more!

Mind maps are not only a tool for putting down your own ideas; they are also an alternative to traditional note-taking. Many people find them easy to study from, as well. Here's how to do it:

1. Write the main idea or section heading from a text in the centre of the page, and draw a circle around it.

2. Now, break that idea down into its parts. Look at the subheadings in the text for clues. Draw lines coming out from the circle and label them in different colours.

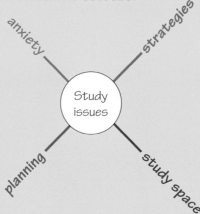

3. For individual facts or ideas, draw lines from the appropriate heading line and label them in the same colour as that heading.

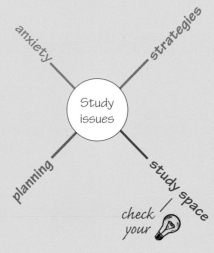

4. Use pictures or symbols that mean something to you to represent important facts or ideas. These will make them more memorable.

Practise the Skill

1. Using several pages from a textbook in another course or this textbook, follow the steps above to take notes on that section.

2. What did you like best about this way of taking notes? What didn't you like? What might you do differently next time?

Empower Yourself

Employability Skills

1. As a business person, you need to be aware of your own skills, but you should also recognize skills and strengths in others. After all, as a business owner or manager, you may need to hire other people to work for you!

   a) With a small group of students, gather around a placemat organizer distributed by your teacher (**Line Master 3-15: Placemat Organizers**).

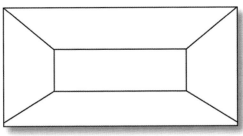

Four-person placemat

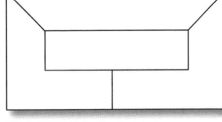

Three-person placemat

   On your own, think of skills that you would want an employee to possess. To give you some ideas, think back to

   - a job interview you had
   - an application you filled out
   - ideas you have heard from your teachers or parents.

   b) On your individual section of the placemat organizer, write down as many point-form skills as you can.

2. As a group, determine the three most important skills an employee should have. Write these "top three employability skills" in the centre of your placemat organizer. Share them orally or by posting them in the classroom so that everyone can walk around and view them.

3. a) As a group, examine your list of employability skills and discuss how you would determine whether a person possessed these skills. Could that person

   - show you the skill?
   - answer an interview question to demonstrate that he or she possessed the skill?
   - bring something to an interview to show that he or she possessed the skill?

   b) On your own, develop a mind map for one of the skills you chose. The mind map should give examples of how a person demonstrates this skill. See the Skills Workshop on page 54 and use ideas from other class members to complete your mind map.

   c) Let all group members review the completed diagrams and add any additional information they think is relevant.

LM 3-16

CHAPTER 4
That's Entertainment

Follow That Wetsuit!

Connect the Text

- What films have you admired for their special effects (FX)?
- Have you tried photo or film editing? What did you do?
- Have you considered studying a communications technology course at your school or at college?

Reading Strategy

1. Before you begin reading, scan the text and note any words that catch your eye. Why did those words attract your interest? How do they help you identify the article topic?
2. Jot down any italicized titles or bolded words that you are familiar with.

Actor Andy Serkis playing Gollum in a motion-capture suit

Gollum brought to life through motion-capture

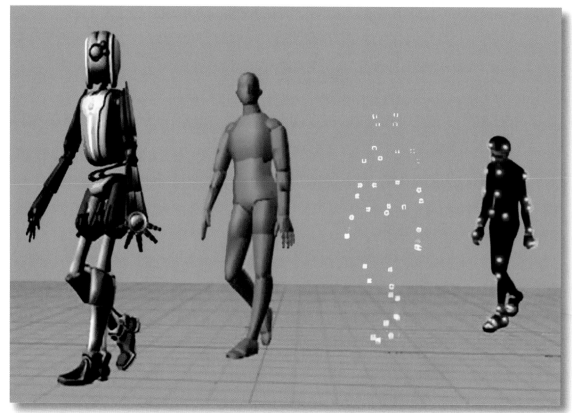

From reflective dots to fantasy character. What kind of film or video game might such a character appear in? How can you tell?

"We looked ridiculous and we felt pretty silly at first." 1

That's how teen actor Spencer Locke (*Monster House, Phil of the Future*) recently described her experience on set with "motion-capture," an **animation** process in which human actors stand in for animation to be used in a film or video game. Why all the silliness? Because actors wear **wetsuits** with reflective dots and act out their scenes in an empty room or stage. Only when all the props and animation have been added does the action make sense. 2

Motion-capture (mo-cap for short) started out as a tool for **engineers**. Now it is used all the time to make fantasy and science-fiction films with eye-popping 3-D characters such as Gollum (from the *Lord of the Rings* trilogy) or King Kong. The characters' actions look real because they are based on human movements. 3

To make motion-capture, filmmakers use computer software to track the reflective dots on the actor's wetsuit. That software can record such **data** as 4

- how fast the person moves
- how quickly the person **accelerates**
- the angle of each body part in motion
- the person's exact dimensions.

All that information and more is stored in the computer and used to make the final animation. The actors' voices and all the scenery are added at the end. The result is not only picture-perfect, but realistic, too. Check out the link below to find out more about motion-capture. 5

Visit **www.emp.ca/ls** to read more information and watch short films about motion-capture and its uses in entertainment, sports, and medicine.

animation
putting pictures together to create the appearance of motion

wetsuits
diving suits

engineers
people who apply science to human needs

data
information

accelerates
increases in speed over time

Read for Meaning

1. Why does the actor say, "We looked ridiculous and we felt pretty silly at first"?
2. Why does the photo on page 56 show four versions of the figure?
3. Use your own words to write a description of motion-capture or to explain it orally to another person.
4. Write at least two questions you would like answered about motion-capture.
5. The title *Follow That Wetsuit!* is a play on words. Can you explain it?

Sharpen Your Writer's Craft

1. How does the bulleted list in paragraph 4 complete the lead-in sentence, "That software can record such data as…"?
2. Why are italics used for some groups of words? How would you show these words if you were writing the article by hand?
3. What is the effect of enclosing some words in parentheses?

Jump In

1. Movies with motion-capture are often very expensive to make. Examine these box office figures for movies that have used motion-capture animation:

Mo-Cap at the Box Office

Movie	Year Released	Estimated Movie Budget*	Box Office Ticket Sales*
Star Wars: Episode 1—The Phantom Menace	1999	$115 000 000	$922 379 000
Lord of the Rings: The Fellowship of the Ring	2001	$109 000 000	$860 700 000
The Polar Express	2004	$170 000 000	$274 871 234

* All amounts shown in US dollars.

a) These amounts are in US dollars (USD). Rewrite this table in Canadian dollars (CAD) using an exchange rate of $1 USD = $1.15 CAD.

b) Which movie on this list made the most money? How much did it make?

c) Which movie on this list made the least money? How much did it make?

d) These three movies are among the highest-earning movies of all time. Why do you think audiences are so attracted to computer-animated movies?

2. A movie made with motion-capture technology may fill hundreds of gigabytes (GB) of storage space on a powerful computer. However, many people measure their data storage needs in megabytes (MB), not gigabytes. Study Table 1 and Table 2. Then answer the questions below.

LM 4-1

Table 1

Device	Gigabytes (GB)
MP3 Music Player	20.0
Digital Camera	1.0
USB Flash Drive	2.0
Notebook Computer	100.0

Table 2

File	Megabytes (MB)
MP3 Song	3.5
JPEG Photo	1.5
2-Minute Video Clip	125.0
3-Page Document	0.04

a) If 1 GB is equal to 1024 MB, calculate the number of megabytes that each device in Table 1 can hold.

b) You have to move the following items from one computer to another:

   i) 300 MP3 songs

   ii) 250 JPEG photographs

   iii) a two-minute video clip

   iv) a dozen three-page documents

   Can you use the USB flash drive to move them all at once? Explain your answer.

3. Actors who work in motion-capture use their own movements, gestures, and facial expressions to tell you something about the mood or attitude of their character. This is called "body language." (See Skills Workshop, page 60.) We use body language every day without thinking about it. Here are some examples:

a) Study each cartoon and explain what each character is communicating through body language.

b) Look at the picture of Gollum on page 56. How does actor Andy Serkis use body language to create the character of Gollum?

c) With a partner, create your own Body Language Dictionary. Use a digital camera to photograph each other in a variety of moods and attitudes (e.g., angry, scared, excited, welcoming). Print each photograph on its own page, and describe the body language shown in the picture.

Making Body Language Work for You

Knowing about body language is the first step toward making it work for you. Body language is talk with your body. It includes the way you are standing or sitting; the gestures you make with your hands or arms; and the expression on your face.

Effective body language works for you. It complements (works with) what you are saying to communicate a total message. Ineffective body language works against you. Ineffective body language can be confusing (your mouth says one thing and your gestures say another) or hostile (you look scary). It can cause people to stop listening altogether.

The Body Language Check List

Here are some pointers on checking or fixing your body language in different situations:

Message Purpose

Check your purpose. Are you offering an apology, complaining to a store manager, or asking your parents for a privilege? Does your body language suit that purpose?

Be the Coach
Jason apologized to Adiba for running her down behind her back. While he apologized, he looked down and folded his arms over his chest. Coach Jason in better body language in this situation.

Message Clarity

Does your body language support what you are saying or contradict it?

Be the Coach
Tara told the manager of her local stationery store that his three-ring binders were defective. While speaking to him, she took a cell phone call, turned away, laughed at the caller's joke, then turned back and said, "So anyway, I hope you will take my complaint seriously." Coach Tara in better body language in this situation.

Message Venue

Are you talking to one person in an informal setting (face to face in the hallway) or to many people in a more formal setting (class presentation)? Gestures should usually be smaller when you are face to face. When you speak to a crowd, your gestures can be bigger.

Be the Coach
At the podium, addressing a school assembly, Ishan keeps his hand gestures about 6 cm off the page, very close to his chest. Coach Ishan in better body language in this situation.

Practise the Skill

With a partner, role-play the following situations using effective body language. One person can do the gestures while the other offers coaching. Then switch roles.

1. Explain to your teacher why you have to hand in your assignment a week late.

2. Ask a parent to extend your curfew so that you can go to a party that "everyone's going to."

3. Apologize for spraying mustard all over the principal's tie in the cafeteria line.

4. Welcome to your school a new student who has come from another country.

Empower Yourself

Empathy, Initiative

1. Spencer Locke says, "We looked ridiculous and we felt pretty silly at first." Thinking by yourself, try to recall a time in your life when you were embarrassed. Decide if you are comfortable sharing this with your classmates.

Bring on the embarrassment!

2. Working in a group of two to five students, share some times in your life when you have been embarrassed or when you saw someone else in an embarrassing situation.

3. Look back to the Body Language Dictionary you created in Jump In (page 59). Is there a picture of a person who is embarrassed?

4. As a group, choose one embarrassing situation that everyone can relate to. Use **Line Master 4-3: Situation Mind Map** to describe how the person in that situation might have felt.

5. Have you ever been embarrassed at school? In class? In your working group, brainstorm a list of all the things that can embarrass students in class. Share your list with the rest of your class by recording your items on a chalkboard or chart paper.

6. In your working group, choose three embarrassing situations that happened to students in class and offer suggestions that would help someone deal with the situation in a positive way. Use **Line Master 4-4: Solutions Chart** to record your work.

7. You are part of a group of teachers and students called MESH (Managing Embarrassing Situations at High School). You are about to visit an elementary school in your neighbourhood. Working individually or in a small group, create a media product designed to help younger students who are just entering high school and are worried about being embarrassed. Your product could be a poster, pamphlet, or PowerPoint presentation.

LM 4-5

Music That's More Than Entertainment

Connect the Text

- Have you ever been involved in raising money for a good cause? What did you do?
- Do you think fundraisers really benefit the people they are meant to help? Why or why not?

Reading Strategy

Read the title of this article. What words tell you that this is not just another article about music or the music industry?

harnessing
directing the force of

Do you love music? Many young people do. By **harnessing** the power of music for three, eight, or even 12 hours, you can raise funds to help children living in a war zone. 1

pledges
promises to pay based on a unit (hour, kilometre)

Keep The Beat is a youth fundraising event sponsored by War Child Canada. As participating students, you get to pick the project and plan the event. You can also raise the money through **pledges**. War Child Canada will support you through their Web site and with **downloadable** materials. Even if you don't know what project you would like to support, War Child Canada can help you decide. 2

downloadable
able to be received over the Internet

One rewarding aspect of raising money for children in war-torn countries is that your dollars go a long way. In Iraq, for example, $100 raised can buy supplies for a whole school for one month. In Ethiopia, the same amount is enough to train a young person struggling to support a family. 3

marathon
any very long event

Whether you hold a small event for a few hours or a schoolwide **marathon** every year, as long as you keep the music playing and do some activity, you're "keeping the beat." Some schools feature live performances on stage; in other schools, students have held **impromptu** gatherings in the hallway, tapping toes or playing drums for minutes or hours. 4

impromptu
without advance preparation

Maria with Dave and Cone

Westdale Secondary School, Hamilton, Ontario

Wondering what the principal will think about the idea? Visit the link below and download the School Support Letter. Want to know what other students have done? Browse the Photo Gallery and Event Activities. Not sure how the event works? The War Child Canada site has all the information you need to hold your own event. If it's a success, you may also be eligible to win prizes. Check out the link below to find out more about War Child Canada and Keep The Beat.

Visit **www.emp.ca/ls** to read more information about holding your own Keep The Beat fundraiser and to download related documents.

Read for Meaning

1. What is the purpose of this article?
2. What is Keep The Beat?
3. How can students harness the power of music to raise funds?
4. What does "your dollars go a long way" mean?
5. What do the following words mean in the context of this article:

   a) marathon?   b) impromptu?
6. What information does the article say is available on the Keep The Beat Web site?

Sharpen Your Writer's Craft

1. Why do you think the article begins with a question? How does this draw the reader in?
2. What is the purpose of all the questions in the last paragraph?
3. Why are capital letters not used in "keeping the beat" in paragraph 4, the way they are in paragraphs 2 and 5?

Drumming to keep
the beat

Empower Yourself

Time Management

1. In order to organize a big event such as a fundraiser, you need to plan and schedule in advance. How effectively do you plan for important things in your life? In Chapter 2, you learned how to make time for your goals and your daily activities. How well are you doing? Could you find the time to plan a big event?

   a) Think for a minute about the systems you use to keep track of time and activities. Share your ideas in a small group or with your whole class. Listen to the ideas of others. Are there any systems other students are using that you could use?

   b) In a group of two to five students, generate a list of things you would like to do that you still can't make time for.

   c) Look at **Line Master 4-9: Tomorrow**. From the list you just created, enter all the things that you could do tomorrow.

   d) Look at **Line Master 4-10: Next Week**. From the list you created in 1b), enter all the things that you could do next week.

   e) Share your planning with your group and do the following check:

   - Do you share a class with anyone in the group? Does that student have any homework or project deadlines recorded that you should too?

   - Does anyone in the class work at the same place as you? Do they have similar shifts?

   - Is anyone in the class in the same clubs or on the same teams as you? Do they have practice, rehearsal, or meeting times that you should enter?

   f) Survey your class and record how many students mentioned the following activities on their planning templates.

   - homework
   - working at a part-time job
   - babysitting
   - relaxing
   - studying
   - playing sports
   - watching television
   - preparing food for family
   - hanging out with friends
   - working out or exercising
   - listening to music
   - finishing a project for school
   - spending time on the computer

2. Do people always plan for the things they think are important in life? As a group, discuss the things that you left off your planning templates but are still important to you.

a) On your own, examine **Line Master 4-11: Next Month**. Start by scheduling the things you know you have to do (school, work, other commitments). Make sure you have noted important events (exams, tests, birthdays) and regular activities (e.g., working out).

b) Now add some things that are important to you and make you happy. How much time do you have left over for the things that are important to you? If you don't have enough time for these activities, what could you change about your current commitments?

c) Use this check list help you decide how to make time for something that is important to you.

Does the activity...

✓ replace an activity you can cut back on?

✗ take time away from something else you know you should be doing?

✓ lead to an important life goal?

✗ represent something that upsets or frustrates others?

✓ represent a commitment you made to yourself or to someone else?

✗ represent something you are doing out of guilt?

✓ make you a happy, well-balanced person?

✗ cause you to put off doing something important?

d) What is the value of noticing how you use your time? How is being more mindful of your time helping you achieve your school and personal goals? Write down your thoughts and place them in your portfolio.

Jump In

1. Neebin is pitching an idea for a new reality TV show to APTN, about surviving in bad weather. She needs your feedback. In her first planned episode, four people and their pilot travelling to a northern First Nations community are stranded when the engine of their single-propeller plane cuts out. Use **Line Master 4-12: Plane Crash Survival** to do this activity.

A single-propeller plane on a frozen lake in northern Ontario

Your teacher will guide you through the following steps:

a) Read the background story that Neebin has written.

b) Form a group of five students. Each group member will play the role of one of the plane crash survivors. As a group, consider two possible survival strategies:

   • Strategy 1: Walk to the nearest community.

   • Strategy 2: Build a shelter and two fires. One fire is for warmth; a second is to signal for help.

   Work together and create a plan for each strategy. How would you do it? What supplies would you use?

c) List the pros and cons for each strategy, thinking about the winter conditions and the personal abilities of each survivor. As a group, come to a consensus about which strategy you will use. Each person in the group must agree on the same strategy. Change your plans as much as needed to make sure everyone agrees.

How to Achieve Consensus

There are lots of ways to make decisions in a group. Have you ever watched kids play Rock-Paper-Scissors to decide who will have the next turn? This is a good example of deciding by chance. In some groups, strong personalities emerge who make decisions for the whole group. This is an example of autocratic decision making, or bossiness.

How is Rock-Paper-Scissors a good way to make decisions? How is it not?

Voting is a popular method of decision making in Canada. So is achieving consensus. These two methods of decision making are not identical. In voting, people have two or more options, for example, candidates for school council or themes for a prom. The option that gets the most votes is the winner.

Consensus works differently. When you achieve consensus on something, you discuss it in detail and everyone agrees at the end of the process. There are no winners or losers. Not everyone will be happy about everything, but everyone's view will have been heard, and all participants will share in the final result.

Sound easy? You'll find out in the following exercise.

1. Build It

Gather with two or three other students around a level surface, such as a desk. Make sure you have on hand:

- 20–30 sheets of construction paper
- scissors
- tape.

Your task is to make the highest possible self-supporting tower, using only the construction paper and tape. You may fold the paper or use scissors to cut it.

2. Debrief It

Don't worry if your tower is not the highest one in the room! The purpose of this activity is to illustrate consensus in action. As a group, consider the following questions. Record your answers on paper.

a) What did you do first?

b) Did anyone make suggestions? What happened then?

c) Was there disagreement? How was it handled?

d) How was everyone persuaded to reach an agreement? Take a poll.

e) What happened once you all agreed on the way to build the tower?

Practise the Skill

Use what you learned about achieving consensus in this exercise and apply it to a situation you have experienced. Describe the situation, and what you did, in your journal. How was it an improvement over the way you might usually handle decision making or disagreement?

The Art of Doodling

Connect the Text

- What is "doodling"? Do you doodle? Do you know others who doodle?
- What questions do you have about doodling and people who doodle?

Reading Strategy

1. Scan the article and take note of its organization. How is it divided?
2. How is the second part of the article different from the first? What can you guess about the first part of the article based on the second part?

brainstorm
to suggest ideas quickly

doodling
drawing without much thinking

graphologists
people who analyze the meaning of handwriting

subconscious
an active part of your mind that you are not aware of

symbols
meaningful images that stand for other things

Manuel and Noor have just spent 10 minutes on the telephone. They are planning a surprise party for a friend and have just begun to **brainstorm** ideas. Although neither is aware that the other is **doodling**, both teens produce interesting doodles: Manuel draws an arrow pointed down. Noor draws a closed book.

1

Doodling is a way to express ideas without words. Because you don't need words to doodle, your mind doesn't have to focus on writing or speaking; instead, it can just move your hand. **Graphologists** think that doodling is driven by your **subconscious** mind. This is the part of your mind that dreams and thinks in **symbols**.

2

What do you think of this doodle?
Do you like it? Why or why not?

What do you think Manuel and Noor's doodles mean? Manuel's doodle could be a symbol for his negative feelings about the surprise party. In fact, Manuel *is* a little angry at his friend because he hasn't returned an expensive DVD in three months. Noor's doodle may show that she is mostly concerned about keeping the party a secret. If she had drawn an open book, it might have revealed her interest in learning more about how to surprise her friend.

3

Using Doodling to Think

You can try doodling to help you be more creative in problem solving. Here's how:

4

1. Think of a problem you have right now. Next, set the problem aside, take a pen and paper, and just draw.

2. Look at what you have drawn. What does it tell you? Don't judge your drawing—just look. Try to see shapes within the shapes. Let your mind wander and see what it comes up with.

3. Ask other people to look at what you have drawn. They may see things that your subconscious is still hiding from you.

Check out the link below to find out more about doodling.

5

Visit **www.emp.ca/ls** to read more about doodling and National Doodle Day, and to view different kinds of doodles.

Read for Meaning

1. According to the article, why do some people doodle?
2. Which of the instructions did you find most useful for doodling? Why?
3. What other ideas might a book symbolize in doodling? Explain your choices.
4. According to the article, what are two good ways to figure out the meaning of your doodles?
5. What type of person do you think is most likely to doodle for fun or to solve problems? Why?

Sharpen Your Writer's Craft

1. Why is the word "neither" in paragraph 1 followed by "is" and not "are"?
2. The second sentence in paragraph 2 begins with the word "because." Prove that it is a complete sentence.
3. How does the prefix "sub" in the word "subconscious" help you understand that word?
4. How does the word "doodling" sound like the activity itself?

CHAPTER 5

Going Green

Get Wise about Hemp

Connect the Text

- What is "hemp"? Find the meaning of the word in a dictionary if you don't know.
- What might you be able to buy in a store that sells only products made from hemp?

Reading Strategy

Complete the first two columns of a KWL chart to record what you know about hemp, and what you would like to find out about it. Complete the third column after reading the text to record what you have learned about this versatile product.

Hey, Janelle

Greenpeace
international
environmental
organization
founded in
Vancouver, BC,
in 1971

I made it to Vancouver! Did you know that **Greenpeace** was founded here back   1
in 1971? Their first protest was against nuclear testing. Now they also work to
protect old forests. Well, today I ran across a store these guys would have loved.

Dayne prepares to e-mail Janelle a picture of the hemp store.

WISE WORDS

"For each of our actions there are only consequences."

— James Lovelock,
British scientist and
environmentalist

Noticed a symbol near the front of the store that I thought was a marijuana leaf. 2
However, this store had nothing to do with drugs. The shop was packed with
clothing, shoes, and body care products such as shampoos and skin conditioners.
I couldn't see how these things related until I got talking with Steve, the store
clerk. Steve explained that all his goods were connected to the hemp plant.

I was surprised to learn that everything in the store was made from hemp. The 3
difference between hemp and marijuana is the level of **THC** (tetrahydrocannabinol),
the stuff that makes you high. Marijuana has a lot of THC, which is why it's illegal;
hemp has almost none. A common mistake is thinking that hemp can make you
high.

Steve told me that hemp is also used to make cookies, sauces, and salad 4
dressings, as well as paint, household detergents, and building materials. For a
long time, hemp was used to make paper, and ropes for ships. Eventually, other
products—like wood and cotton—replaced it because of their superior qualities.

So why grow hemp at all? The answer takes us back to all those environmentalists 5
who started making waves back in the 1960s and 1970s. They got people thinking
about the need to protect the environment.

Hemp's defenders say that it causes less harm to the environment. Making paper 6
from wood pulp causes **deforestation**, but hemp grows fast. It also doesn't need
the chemical bleaching that wood pulp does to turn it into paper. Growing hemp
also doesn't require lots of water or **pesticides**.

Anyway, I gotta dash. But now that I've got your interest, check out my photos 7
and the link and see for yourself!

Dayne

Visit **www.emp.ca/ls** to learn more about hemp and its uses.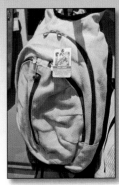

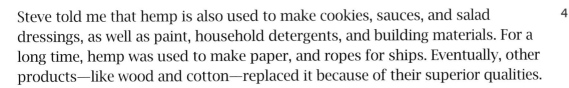
A hemp knapsack

THC
chemical that
makes you high
and reduces
inhibitions
(feelings that
hold you back)

deforestation
large-scale
cutting down and
removal of trees

pesticides
substances used
to kill plant,
animal, and
insect pests

Read for Meaning
1. How are the first and last paragraphs of this text connected?
2. Why would environmentalists have liked this store?
3. Why was Dayne confused about the source of the products?
4. According to the text, how is hemp friendly to the environment?

Sharpen Your Writer's Craft
1. Is this text an e-mail or a handwritten letter? How do you know?
2. This message is obviously intended for a friend because of the informal style
   of language used. Quote as many examples of informal language used in this
   text as you can find. Use **Line Master 3-4: Elements of a News Story** for tips
   on newspaper style.
3. Rewrite paragraph 1, 2, or 3 using the style of a newspaper article intending
   to inform readers about hemp.

Jump In

1. Write a reply e-mail to Dayne. In your e-mail
   a) thank him for writing
   b) wish him well on his vacation
   c) ask him two questions about hemp that he can answer for you by visiting the hemp store.

2. Design your own catalogue to advertise different hemp products. Tip: Get some ideas by looking at the catalogue sample on the opposite page. Your catalogue should include
   a) a picture of each product
   b) a description of each product
   c) the environmental benefits of each product
   d) a price for each product.

   Use an Internet search engine to help you find images and information about your products. Write a draft of your catalogue with **Line Master 5-1: Hemp Product Catalogue**, and then make a final copy using word-processing or publishing software.

celebrity endorsement
statement by a famous person that a product is excellent

3. Write a **celebrity endorsement** of a hemp product. Begin by choosing a celebrity that you admire, and a hemp product that you would find useful. In several sentences, write what that celebrity might say to convince people to buy the product.

The Foo Fighters have used hemp-blend paper for their CD inserts.

4. Brianna is shopping for hemp products using an online catalogue. She would like to buy the following items:

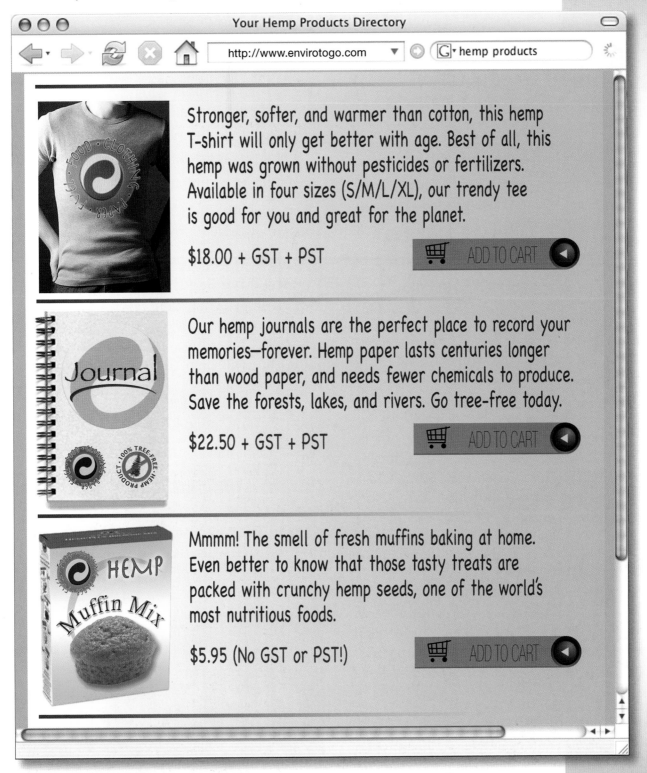

Your Hemp Products Directory

http://www.envirotogo.com   hemp products

Stronger, softer, and warmer than cotton, this hemp T-shirt will only get better with age. Best of all, this hemp was grown without pesticides or fertilizers. Available in four sizes (S/M/L/XL), our trendy tee is good for you and great for the planet.

$18.00 + GST + PST   ADD TO CART

Our hemp journals are the perfect place to record your memories—forever. Hemp paper lasts centuries longer than wood paper, and needs fewer chemicals to produce. Save the forests, lakes, and rivers. Go tree-free today.

$22.50 + GST + PST   ADD TO CART

Mmmm! The smell of fresh muffins baking at home. Even better to know that those tasty treats are packed with crunchy hemp seeds, one of the world's most nutritious foods.

$5.95 (No GST or PST!)   ADD TO CART

a) Make a list of the environmental benefits of these hemp products.

b) In what ways are these products superior to those made without hemp?

c) Find the cost of each product, including sales taxes.

d) If the company charges $7.50 for shipping and handling, what is the grand total of Brianna's bill?

How to Talk and Listen in a Small Group

Communicating in a small group can be challenging. There are natural talkers who talk a lot and never seem to listen. There are shy people who talk too little. And then there are people who often tune out completely. They are too bored to talk or listen. How can a group like this have a discussion or get anything done?

Tall Tips for Small Groups

1. Give Everyone Time
At the start of a discussion, let everyone contribute at least one idea. This makes it less likely for people to fade out later.

2. Have a Moderator
Appoint someone the moderator of the discussion. A moderated discussion means that everyone has a chance to talk and listen. See **Line Master 5-2: Moderator Do's and Don'ts** for more information on the role of the moderator.

3. State, Don't Harp
When you have made your point, try to avoid repeating it. Sometimes it's a good idea to conclude your remarks with, "That's been my experience. Anyone else want to jump in?" This question encourages someone else to contribute.

4. Let People Think Out Loud
Many people think best when talking. When someone seems to be working an idea, let that person do that. You may hear pauses or see body language that says the person is thinking. Don't jump in with a response right away; let the speaker finish.

5. Build on Other People's Ideas
Great ideas are often built as a team. When you hear an idea that catches your interest, try these piggy backers:

- "Hey, that reminds me—"
- "Right, and we could also—"
- "I heard a similar story—"

These piggy backers extend the discussion and usually make it more enjoyable.

6. Give and Receive Constructive Feedback
Stay positive when you offer feedback on someone's idea and when someone responds to yours. When offering feedback, say something that will help the person develop an idea. Avoid attacks.

No: "Your idea sucks."

Yes: "I think people need to hear more details."

Practise the Skill
Use what you learned in this Skills Workshop in your next small-group discussion. How did following these tips make the discussion better? Which tip did you find most helpful? Why?

Empower Yourself

Initiative

1. The text "Get Wise about Hemp" mentions that environmentalists got people thinking about the need to protect the earth. The hemp store sells:

cookies   paint

sauces   household detergents

salad dressings   building materials

paper   ropes

As a class, brainstorm how these products can sometimes have a harmful impact on the environment. Think about how these products are produced, used, and disposed of. Keep track of your list on a chalkboard or sheet of chart paper.

2. Form a group of two to five students. Each person will need a copy of **Line Master 5-3: Healthy Environments Organizer**. What products, industries, or other activities are harmful to the environment at home, at school, and at work? List these factors at the top of **Line Master 5-3**.

3. Your physical environment isn't the only thing that can affect your health and well-being. Sometimes an environment can be socially or emotionally toxic.

   a) As a class, discuss what it means to be in a socially or emotionally toxic environment.

   b) In your working group, discuss what kinds of things might be polluting your social or emotional environment at home, school, or work. Individually, complete the second part of **Line Master 5-3: Healthy Environments Organizer**.

   c) In your group, discuss whether or not you have ever harmed the physical environment or made someone else's social-emotional environment unpleasant. You might choose to share some examples in your group.

   d) In your group, think of different positive actions you could take to improve the environments in which you live, go to school, and work. These can be small actions, like smiling at someone in the school hallway or throwing trash into a trash can instead of littering.

   e) On your own, commit to taking one action to improve the physical environment and one thing to improve the social-emotional environment. Record your commitments at the bottom of **Line Master 5-3**. You may also want to write yourself a reminder note in your agenda.

The Power of One

Connect the Text

■ List some memorable trips you have experienced. What made you remember them?

■ Do you follow the national and international news? What issues interest you? Why?

Reading Strategy

After reading the preamble to the article (shown below in italics), predict examples of events that led to Simon's passion. At the end of the reading, note how any of your predictions were accurate.

Simon Jackson is the founder and executive director of the Spirit Bear Youth Coalition. This organization works to protect the habitat of a rare white bear, the Kermode bear of British Columbia, also called the Spirit Bear. In this article, Simon reflects on some of the events that led to his passion.

The greatest gift my parents ever gave me was the gift of travel. We didn't visit the **exotic** wonders of the world or the sunny beaches of Mexico or Hawaii. Instead, we packed up our car every summer and drove—across Canada, to Alaska, or through the American Southwest. ¹

exotic
unusual and mysterious

A grizzly mother with her cubs. Grizzly bears are native to the northwestern United States and Canada.

Each of these trips allowed for my young and curious mind to learn all about our own North American backyard. On one such trip our final stop was Yellowstone National Park, an **untouched wilderness** in northwestern Wyoming. It was there that I saw my first wild bear—a mother grizzly with two cubs—in a meadow about 1 kilometre from the road. It was a sight that captured my imagination and my curiosity. A passion was born. 2

Television news was served up every evening with dinner in my family. During one such newscast, I saw a story about the Kodiak bears in Alaska and the plans being drawn up that would threaten their future. When I heard the news, my seven-year-old mind saw it as an assault on the very same bears I had just seen in Yellowstone. I became determined to help. 3

My parents were hardly **activists** but when I asked what I could do, they suggested writing letters or raising money: I decided to do both. Like any seven-year-old growing up in Vancouver, lemonade stands were a **staple** of my summer months, so it made perfect sense to have a lemonade stand that would raise money for the Kodiak bears. I raised $60 and wrote letters to then–Prime Minister Brian Mulroney and then-President George Bush Sr. 4

Two months after my first **foray** into the world of "activism," I received a letter in the mail announcing that the Kodiak bears were saved. I was certain that my $60 and two letters had saved them. Although I realized later that this wasn't the case, I also learned something important: one person can make a difference for all life. 5

This gift of hope also taught me that I could do the same thing for other animals, for other issues. It was a powerful tool that would allow me to overcome the many obstacles I would soon face in my quest to save another bear—the Spirit Bear. 6

Visit **www.emp.ca/ls** to read more about the Spirit Bear Youth Coalition and its campaign to save the Spirit Bear.

untouched wilderness
an area with no development

activists
people who work for a cause

staple
everyday item you use

foray
entrance into

Read for Meaning

1. Explain how the author sees travel as a "gift" from his parents.
2. How can an area be described as an "untouched wilderness" when it is a popular tourist destination?
3. "Television news was served up every night with dinner in my family." Did the family actually serve the news at the table? Explain.
4. What is unusual about the closing sentence of the article? How does it affect the reader?

Sharpen Your Writer's Craft

1. What is the purpose of the preamble? How is it different from the rest of the text?
2. Explain the use of dashes in this sentence in paragraph 2: "It was there that I saw …". What other punctuation could be used instead?
3. Create a different title for this article. Explain your choice.

CHAPTER 6
Stand Up, Speak Up

When Relationships Go Bad

Connect the Text

■ People need relationships, but sometimes they turn sour. Jot down five characteristics of a healthy relationship. It can be any kind of relationship—not just a romantic one.

Reading Strategy

These words and phrases are all from the article below. What might this article be about?

addicted	married	losers	silent treatment
Dear Desperate	counsellor	free to be yourself	See ya

Dear Miz No2Much:

addicted
emotionally
or physically
dependent on
someone or
something

My girlfriend and I are so in love, it's like we're **addicted**. We're even talking about getting married. The problem is we're starting to fight a lot. And when we fight, she knows just what to say to hurt me. She's been after me to drop some of my friends because they're "losers." I don't know what to do. I need her but I've never felt so lousy.

Desperate in Kingston

Dear Desperate,

2

Here's a 10-point check list to test the health of your relationship. For each point, give yourself a green light if this is not a problem, an amber light if you have some concerns, and a red light if this is a major issue.

Your partner

1. is always putting you down or finding fault with your family or friends. 3
2. blames you for problems in your relationship.
3. has threatened violence or has **abused** you physically.
4. pressures you to do things you don't want to do.
5. is often **suspicious** or jealous—doesn't want you hanging around with others.
6. wrongly accuses you of doing bad things or thinking bad thoughts.
7. lies to you or hides things from you.
8. has sudden **mood swings** without any obvious reason.
9. demands your constant attention but doesn't consider your needs or wants.
10. likes to play **mind games**, like giving you the **silent treatment**.

If more than one or two ambers or reds show up, consider doing the following: 4

- Talk to a person you trust—a friend or a family member.
- End the relationship.
- If you are depressed, talk to a counsellor.
- Check out the link below.

The bottom line is, if you don't feel safe or free to be yourself, it's time to say "See ya." 5

Visit **www.emp.ca/ls** to read more advice on handling relationships and getting out of an unhealthy one.

abused
mistreated in a physical or emotional way

suspicious
assumes bad things about someone or something

mood swings
extreme changes in mood; e.g., from happy to sad

mind games
acting in a way to confuse or manipulate someone

silent treatment
not speaking to someone to show anger

Read for Meaning

1. Look again at the five-point list you created under Connect the Text. For each point, find a quotation from the article to prove that an unhealthy relationship is the exact opposite of a healthy one.
2. Quote a word from the article that indicates that Desperate and his girlfriend need to be together all the time.
3. Quote a phrase from the article that proves that Desperate is very unhappy in this relationship.
4. Explain the meaning of the following expressions: mood swings; mind games; silent treatment. Show your understanding by giving an example of each.
5. Do you think that Desperate should marry his girlfriend? Give a detailed reason for your answer.
6. Read the Wise Words. Explain the imagery that Woody Allen uses in the movie *Annie Hall* by calling his relationship with his girlfriend "a dead shark."

WISE WORDS

"A relationship, I think, is like a shark. It has to constantly move forward or it dies. And I think what we've got on our hands is a dead shark."

— *Woody Allen, Annie Hall*

Sharpen Your Writer's Craft

1. Read Miz No2Much's advice to Desperate again. In a small group, discuss which items on her check list you agree with or disagree with.

2. Now pretend that you are Miz No2Much and write your own advice to Desperate. It can be in paragraph format. Keep it short and to the point. Limit yourself to approximately 10 lines.

3. a) Share your advice with your classmates. Ask them what they think about your advice.

   b) Whose advice do they prefer—yours or that of Miz No2Much? Why?

Jump In

1. In any relationship between two people, it can be difficult to discuss a problem without sounding like you are blaming or judging. "I" statements instead of "You" statements are a good way to get your point across in a positive way.

   a) Read and study the examples below.

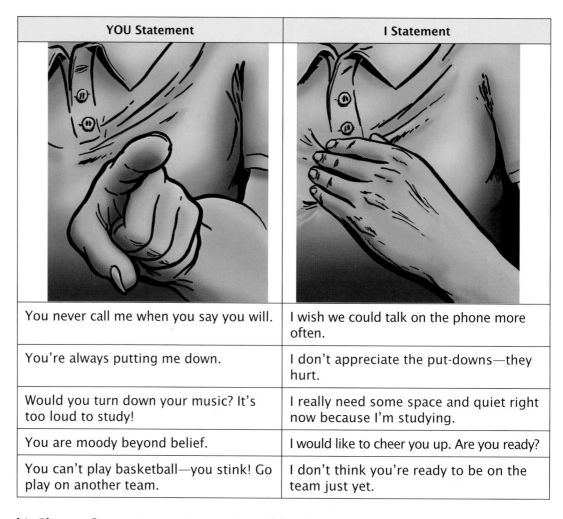

YOU Statement	I Statement
You never call me when you say you will.	I wish we could talk on the phone more often.
You're always putting me down.	I don't appreciate the put-downs—they hurt.
Would you turn down your music? It's too loud to study!	I really need some space and quiet right now because I'm studying.
You are moody beyond belief.	I would like to cheer you up. Are you ready?
You can't play basketball—you stink! Go play on another team.	I don't think you're ready to be on the team just yet.

   b) Choose five points on Miz No2Much's relationship check list (page 101). For each point, write an "I" statement that could be used to start a conversation about that problem.

2. Pat and Robin are in a relationship and have been fighting a lot lately. To help them get back on track, they have decided to take a fun trip together to the city on Saturday. Examine the schedule below to help them make plans.

Lakeshore East GO Train
Oshawa–Whitby–Ajax–Pickering–Toronto

Saturday, Sunday, and Holidays

Westbound

TRIP NUMBER	Oshawa GO	Whitby GO	Ajax GO	Pickering GO	Rouge Hill GO	Guildwood GO	Eglinton GO	Scarborough GO	Danforth GO	Toronto Union Station
905	06 41	06 47	06 54	07 00	07 07	07 13	07 18	07 22	07 27	07 37
907	07 41	07 47	07 54	08 00	08 07	08 13	08 18	08 22	08 27	08 37
909	08 41	08 47	08 54	09 00	09 07	09 13	09 18	09 22	09 27	09 37
911	09 41	09 47	09 54	10 00	10 07	10 13	10 18	10 22	10 27	10 37

Eastbound

TRIP NUMBER	Toronto Union Station	Danforth GO	Scarborough GO	Eglinton GO	Guildwood GO	Rouge Hill GO	Pickering GO	Ajax GO	Whitby GO	Oshawa GO
926	18 13	18 23	18 29	18 33	18 37	18 42	18 49	18 54	19 01	19 08
928	19 13	19 23	19 29	19 33	19 37	19 42	19 49	19 54	20 01	20 08
930	20 13	20 23	20 29	20 33	20 37	20 42	20 49	20 54	21 01	21 08
932	21 13	21 23	21 29	21 33	21 37	21 42	21 49	21 54	22 01	22 08
934	22 13	22 23	22 29	22 33	22 37	22 42	22 49	22 54	23 01	23 08

a) How long will it take Pat and Robin to travel from Oshawa, where they live, to Union Station in downtown Toronto?

b) Use **Line Master 6-1: Take the Train to the City** to create a plan for Pat and Robin's day trip. Your itinerary should contain the following information:
- the departure times and trip numbers of the two trains they will take
- their meal, shopping, and movie plans
- your suggestions for other activities they can do in Toronto.

How to Solve a Problem

What does a relationship have to do with math? Each can be posed in the form of a problem. Believe it or not, you can use the same problem-solving techniques in both situations.

1. Problem-solving always begins with what you know. What do you really know about your problem? Figure out the big things you know and the small things you know. These are like the main ideas and the less important ideas of a paragraph or essay. Write them down.

Big Things	Less Important Things

2. How do you know those things? Write down your reasons, or evidence. Here's an example: Ned knows that Clara plans to cheat on her English test. He knows because Clara showed him how she intends to do it.

What I Know	My Evidence

3. Throw out information that isn't about the problem. For example, if you know that you will be late with a major assignment, forget about whether you'll wear the blue shirt or the beige one when you inform your teacher.

4. Say, "This is like the time—" Try to think of another problem like this one. How was it resolved?

5. Use your preferred learning style (see pages 8–10). For example, represent the problem in pictures, as a 3-D model, or as a story. Using your learning style to represent the problem in a way that makes sense to you can help you achieve a breakthrough.

6. Think of all the questions you have about the problem. Get clarification from someone else, such as a teacher, or clarify your own thinking. For example, Ned had to clarify in his own mind that Clara was wrong to cheat even if she had been sick before the test.

7. State the problem to yourself using your own words. Use everything you know in order to solve that problem. If you still can't solve it, go back over the steps and fill in any blanks.

Practise the Skill

1. Using **Line Master 6-2: Math Problem** and **Line Master 6-3: Relationship Problem**, try to solve each problem using the steps outlined in this Skills Workshop.

2. a) When you have finished the problem-solving activities, write down two things about the problems that were similar.

   b) What have you learned about your ability to problem-solve?

   c) How can you apply the steps to problem-solving in a school situation this week?

Empower Yourself

Empathy, Initiative

1. Sometimes when people need help, they have a hard time figuring out how to accept assistance.

    a) The article provides some links to organizations that support adolescents. As a class, make a list of people, supports, and organizations that exist within your school and community. List these on the chalkboard or on chart paper.

    b) Toxic relationships (relationships that poison) are not limited to romantic relationships. As a class, list other kinds of relationships that can become unhealthy.

    c) On your own, ask yourself if you have ever known anyone in an unhealthy relationship. You may wish to keep your thoughts private at this time.

2. a) In a small group of two to five students, review Miz No2Much's 10 symptoms of an unhealthy relationship (page 101). Decide whether there are other symptoms that need to be added to the list. Record them in the centre of **Line Master 6-4: Relationship Mind Map**.

    b) In your working group, think about the reasons that people stay in unhealthy relationships. Try not to "blame the victim"; instead, try to understand his or her fears and circumstances. Record your thoughts on **Line Master 6-4**.

    c) Look carefully at the reasons why people stay in unhealthy relationships. Brainstorm supports that would be useful to help those people. Record these on **Line Master 6-4**.

3. a) Sometimes, well-meaning friends and family try to persuade a person to leave an unhealthy relationship by making comments that really aren't that helpful, such as, "We never liked her, anyway." Brainstorm some actions that are well intentioned but not helpful to a person in a toxic relationship.

    b) On your own, examine the relationship mind map your group created in activity 2, above. Write an e-mail to a person you are trying to support in leaving an unhealthy relationship. The person does not have to be real, but be sure to include realistic and helpful advice and resources.

Diary of a 30-Hour Famine

Connect the Text

- What stories or news have you heard about famine? What are the usual causes of famine?
- What images come to mind?

Reading Strategy

As you read, imagine the words that are in *italics*. When you see these words, stop reading for a moment to engage one or more of your senses: smell (inhale and imagine); sight (close your eyes and imagine); sound (listen and imagine); taste (touch your tongue to your lips and imagine); and touch (touch your skin and imagine).

March 3, 9:00 p.m.

We watched a DVD today of people living in *West Africa*. They were *so skinny* from **malnutrition**. It just seems so hopeless for them. I mean, what can I do to help them? 1

Our teacher mentioned a fundraising event where we don't eat anything for 30 hours. The money we raise will help people like those in the DVD. We get to *sleep over at school, watch movies, and play sports*. So I'm going to sign up. 2

March 12, 7:45 a.m.

Our 30-hour **famine** started officially at 2 o'clock this morning. I must have eaten *a whole pizza* last night so I wouldn't be hungry today. Forty of us signed up and we're all excited to spend the night at the school. We're allowed *juice and water*, but no food. 3

malnutrition
state of not being properly fed; lacking protein and vitamins

famine
extreme shortage of food

WISE WORDS

"If you can't feed a hundred people, then just feed one."
— *Mother Teresa*

Each spring, thousands of Canadian youth give up food for 30 hours to raise money for children around the world.

Some of us were talking about the DVD of the family in Senegal and how we can eat whenever we want. I guess going 30 hours without eating isn't too much for me to give up, especially since I'll be helping someone in need.

4

March 12, 4:00 p.m.

The award-winning *Hotel Rwanda*

We *played basketball and ran through the halls without anyone bugging us.* It was neat hanging out without anybody else around. Then we watched *Hotel Rwanda.* It was a very good movie, really sad, and based on a true story. I can't believe all the people who died in the **genocide**, and those who lived *suffered from disease* with no doctors or hospitals to help them.

5

After the movie, we were talking about how nobody likes to be **lectured**, and that it feels so good to be doing something rather than just telling people that poverty is bad.

6

genocide
mass killing of people belonging to a race or nation

lectured
told what is right for them

March 12, 10:00 p.m.

Not eating dinner was the toughest part of today. After *playing basketball and running in the halls, we were all starving!* But then the hunger passed and we were just *tired and felt weak, like we had no energy.*

7

March 13, 9:00 a.m.

I survived! We *slept in the library* and woke up to the *smell of pancakes and maple syrup.* I didn't realize how hungry I was until I smelled the food. While we were eating, the teacher told us we raised $1600! *Someone from the newspaper came and interviewed us and took our picture, too.*

8

We're already planning next year's 30-hour famine. It's an amazing cause, and it was so good to see everyone come together to help benefit others. It wasn't that hard to give up eating for 30 hours knowing that some people don't have that **luxury**.

9

luxury
something nice to have that is not needed

Visit **www.emp.ca/ls** to find out more about doing the 30-hour famine for World Vision.

Read for Meaning

1. a) What images from the diary were most vivid for you? Why?
   b) How did using your senses affect your reading experience?
2. What do you know about the country of Rwanda? How does the film *Hotel Rwanda* seem to compare with the movies you usually see?
3. Why is a 30-hour famine not much of a challenge? What word in the text sums this up?
4. Why did the students also learn about poverty and genocide during the famine?
5. In your own words, describe a 30-hour famine.

Sharpen Your Writer's Craft

1. About how old do you think the diary writer is? Give reasons for your answer.
2. Is there a specific audience for this diary? Explain your answer.
3. Does this diary excerpt encourage you to try a 30-hour famine? Explain, using specific references to the text.
4. Would you like to read more journal entries on another topic by the same writer? Why or why not?
5. Design a symbol or a poster for a 30-hour famine at your school.

Jump In

1. Lacey is planning to make a pancake breakfast for everyone who participated in her school's 30-hour famine. She found an old recipe of her grandmother's that uses **cups**. She needs to make enough to serve 35 hungry students and teachers.

cup
1 cup = 0.2 litres

Good Old Fashioned Pancakes

Ingredients
1 ½ cups all-purpose flour
3 ½ teaspoons baking powder
1 teaspoon salt
1 tablespoon white sugar
1 ¼ cups milk
1 egg
3 tablespoons butter, melted

Serves 8

Directions

In large bowl, sift together the flour, baking powder, salt, and sugar.

Make a well in the centre and pour in the milk, egg, and melted butter; mix until smooth.

Heat a lightly oiled griddle or frying pan over medium-high heat.

Pour or scoop the batter onto the griddle using approximately ¼ cup for each pancake.

Brown on both sides and serve hot.

a) If this recipe serves eight people, how many times should Lacey increase the recipe? She would like to have some extra servings on hand.
b) Multiply the recipe quantities by the number you found in activity 1a), above. Rewrite the recipe ingredient list, showing the new quantities.

2. In Canada there is more than enough food to go around. However, you can still eat poorly if you do not choose a balanced diet. How balanced is your diet? Use **Line Master 6-5: 24-Hour Nutrition Journal** to keep track of what you eat over the next day. When the time is up, answer these questions:

a) Find the total number of servings you ate in each food group.

b) Were you far off the Canada's Food Guide recommendations? Write a paragraph to answer this question. Use the information you recorded in your nutrition journal to support your answer. (See page 26 to access Canada's Food Guide.)

c) Plan what you will eat for the next 24 hours using **Line Master 6-6: My Nutrition Plan**. Include three meals and several healthy snacks. Aim to eat the recommended number of servings in each food group.

Keeping a food diary is a popular method of determining exactly what you eat and when. How do you shape up?

Sam's Food Diary

Time	Food eaten	Food group and number of servings					How I felt
12:10	sandwich: 2 slices cheese, lettuce and tomato on brown bread	2	1	1			– good sandwich – still hungry – will buy apple in cafeteria

 = grains   = fruit and vegetables

 = dairy   = meat and alternatives   = snack food

This is how Sam's food diary started.

Beating the Odds

Connect the Text

- What do the following conditions have in common: ADHD; dyslexia; hyperactivity?
- Do you know of anybody who has any of the above? What can you tell about that person?

Reading Strategy

Copy the organizer below into your notebook. Decide whether you agree or disagree with the statements in the second column before reading the article. Circle your choice in the first column. Add your proof in the third column.

Before Reading	Statements	My Proof/ Paragraph No.	After Reading
Agree/Disagree	People who dislike reading, writing, and math can't have a successful career.		Agree/Disagree
Agree/Disagree	People with a learning disability can use their own strengths and the strengths of others to achieve success.		Agree/Disagree
Agree/Disagree	If you have a learning disability, you have to try extra hard to overcome barriers.		Agree/Disagree

hyperactive
easily excited; has difficulty sitting still

dyslexic
has difficulty reading print

learning disability
disability that often involves spoken language or print

Meet Paul Orfalea. He bills himself as "a **hyperactive dyslexic** who failed two grades, opened a small copy shop called Kinko's in 1970, and turned it into a $2 billion-a-year company." The punch line? He did it all "while barely being able to read and write." 1

Orfalea's gift was being able to see business opportunities that others couldn't, knowing his strengths, and building on the talents of his employees. He once said, "I can't read well. I really don't know how to run the machines at Kinko's. But I was always looking at what came out of the machine and I knew how to sell it." 2

Orfalea and millions like him have a **learning disability** that makes school a challenge but needn't interfere with their ultimate success. 3

Take Keira Knightley, who struggled with reading and arithmetic as a child because she had dyslexia. She tried to hide her problems by memorizing book tapes, but was still called "stupid" by her classmates. That still didn't stop her from becoming a famous movie star, acting in films such as *Bend It Like Beckham, Pirates of the Caribbean: The Curse of the Black Pearl*, and *Pride and Prejudice*. 4

When Knightley was diagnosed with dyslexia at age six, she was already keenly interested in acting. So her mother made her a deal: Keira could have a talent agent if she spent an extra hour each day of the summer holidays on reading and math. To the surprise of everyone, Keira kept her end of the bargain, and her mother did too. Knightley's television **debut** was one year later.

5

debut
first-time
appearance

Then there's Chris Kaman. At 2 m, 13 cm, this National Basketball Association (NBA) centre is definitely noticeable. He's widely praised for his quickness and the way he studies the game. But it wasn't always so rosy for Kaman. While working steadily to improve his game, Kaman must still deal with the **ADHD (attention-deficit hyperactivity disorder)** he has had since childhood.

6

ADHD
disability that
makes paying
attention and
thinking things
through difficult

"I was just real wild," Kaman said. "Wherever trouble was, I found it—taking people's bikes and putting them on railroad tracks, climbing on neighbours' roofs and having shingle fights back and forth. Just crazy stuff.

7

"When I'd come home, my parents really couldn't control me as well as they wanted, so they made me see somebody and I found out I had ADHD."

8

Kaman finds that his biggest problem is when he's in **huddles**. When he's listening to the coach going over the plays, he has to fight to keep his mind from wandering. He keeps his focus by asking lots of questions and reminding himself that it's better to know "what's going on before it happens."

9

huddle
gathering of the
team to go over
the next plays

Orfalea, Knightley, and Kaman share something in common—a belief that they can make it work, even if they have to go that extra step. Lineman **Mike Lorenz** has said it best: "My whole goal was to play football and play in the NFL. So I'm living my dream and … I'm putting extra effort in to overcome it [dyslexia]. That's what you gotta do in that situation. To anyone out there with a disability, you have to go beyond what's normal."

10

To read more about successful people with disabilities, check out the link below.

11

Visit **www.emp.ca/ls** to read more profiles of successful people with learning disabilities and how they cope.

Chris Kaman and Keira Knightley have overcome learning disabilities and become successful in their respective careers.

WISE WORDS

"We are not lazy, crazy, or stupid."
— *Slogan of an ADHD support group*

Read for Meaning

LM 6-9

1. Have another look at the chart you filled out before reading the article. Does the text agree with you? In the third column, write the paragraph number from the article that shows agreement or disagreement. Circle Agree or Disagree in the last column. Then, copy and complete the graphic organizer below in your notebook.

	Disability	Difficulty That Person Has	Successes That Person Has
Paul Orfalea			
Keira Knightley			
Chris Kaman			

2. Why do you think Paul Orfalea is so successful in business?

3. Approximately how old must Keira Knightley have been when she made her television debut?

4. Has Chris Kaman outgrown his disability? Find proof in the article to back up your answer.

5. What coping strategy does Kaman use to help him focus during huddles?

6. Who is Mark Lorenz? What does he have in common with the other three people mentioned in the article?

7. What is implied by the slogan of the ADHD support group (Wise Words, page 113): "We are not lazy, crazy, or stupid"?

Sharpen Your Writer's Craft

1. What is a "punch line"? Why is the punch line about Paul Orfalea (paragraph 1, lines 3 and 4) effective?

2. In paragraph 4, why is the word "stupid" written in quotation marks?

3. Choose one of the statements in the Reading Strategy organizer (page 112). Write an opinion paragraph of approximately 12 lines in which you clearly explain why you agree or disagree with the statement. Remember to start with a strong opening argument, two or three reasons for your argument, and a final sentence to sum up. For extra strength, invent a punch line of your own that fits your argument.

How to Make a Good Argument

An argument is made up of two parts:

1. a claim   2. evidence

The *claim* part of the argument is where you get to state what you think. It is your opinion. Try not to think of claims as right or wrong, even if they arouse your feelings. Instead, think of them as strong or weak. Claims backed up by strong evidence turn into strong arguments. Similarly, claims backed up by flimsy evidence—or no evidence at all—remain weak arguments.

A claim sounds like this:

- People without disabilities ought to try one on for a week.
- People who refuse to recycle should be fined.
- At sporting events, parents should be discouraged from yelling at kids on the other team.

Evidence follows the claim with the word "because." When you hear that word, you know that the claim is about to be backed up by evidence, or reasons.

Evidence sounds like the parts of these statements shown in italics:

- People without disabilities ought to try one on for a week *because that way, they might learn not to judge someone with a disability.*
- People who refuse to recycle should be fined *because the earth is running out of space for all our garbage.*
- At sporting events, parents should be discouraged from yelling at kids on the other team *because bullying behaviour like that is a bad example for the players.*

Reasons Aren't All Equal

When you are thinking of a reason to back your claim, make sure it's a good reason. Avoid the bad reasons described below.

Top 5 Bad Reasons

1. "Because they're girls (boys, silly, rich, mean, etc.)." (attacking the other person)
2. "Because it's always been done that way." (assuming tradition is always good)
3. "Because they could make trouble." (appealing to fear)
4. "Because everybody does it." (assuming that what everybody does is right)
5. "Because this will happen." (pretending to know with certainty that something will occur)

Practise the Skill

Select one of the claims on the left and create more good reasons to agree with it or to disagree with it. Avoid using bad reasons.

Arguing doesn't have to mean fighting!

Jump In

1. a) "Going the extra step" to succeed can sometimes be very hard. However, the results can be so much better. Jamie's teacher has asked the students to write down instructions for a group of youngsters on making a peanut butter and jam sandwich. Everyone thinks it's pretty easy, including Jamie. Study what Jamie wrote on the left and look at the results on the right.

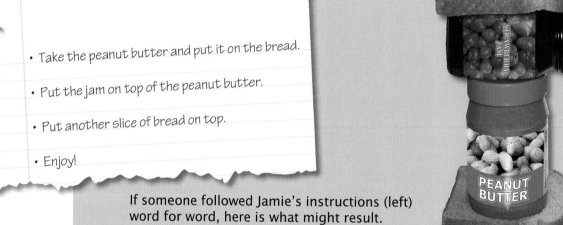

- Take the peanut butter and put it on the bread.
- Put the jam on top of the peanut butter.
- Put another slice of bread on top.
- Enjoy!

If someone followed Jamie's instructions (left) word for word, here is what might result.

What a disaster! That's not a sandwich. So Jamie has tried again. This time he takes that extra step, making sure everything is explained carefully.

1. Open the peanut butter jar and the jam jar.
2. Using a knife, spread a small amount of peanut butter evenly across one slice of bread.
3. Place a small spoonful of jam on a second slice of bread. With the knife, spread the jam evenly over the bread.
4. Put the two pieces of bread together so that the jam side of one slice is facing the peanut butter side of the other slice.
5. Lay the sandwich flat on a plate and cut it in half with the knife from corner to corner.
6. Enjoy!

Now, that's a peanut butter and jam sandwich. Much better!

b) Your secret twin will take your place for a week. He or she must act just like you! Write instructions for a task that you do every day, such as putting on your shoes, making your breakfast, or walking the dog. Your paragraph should

- begin by stating what the instructions are for
- explain clearly how to do each part of the task
- use linking words like "first," "second," "then," and "next" to show the correct order.

2. The old saying "Practice makes perfect" is true for everyone with or without a learning disability. Here is a good way to practise your mental math and build up the "math muscle" you need to succeed. Use **Line Master 6-10: Mental Math Concentration Cards** to create your own game of Concentration. Make sure to create math problems that are not too easy for you!

How to Play

1. Lay out the cards face down with the problems on the left and the answers on the right (see picture below).

2. Turn over a card on the left and then one on the right.

3. If the answer is the correct one for the problem, then remove both cards from the game. If the answer is not the correct one, turn over both cards.

4. Start again at step 2. Concentrate! Continue until all the problem cards have been matched with their answers.

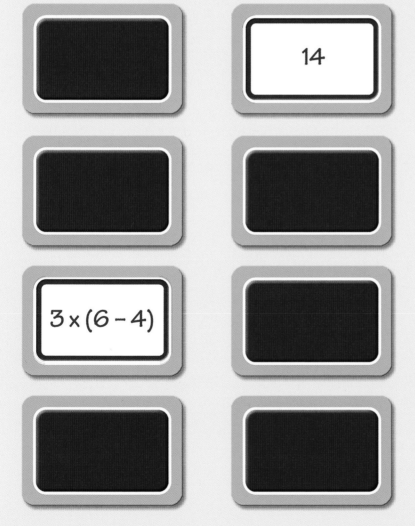

Ayeesha turned over these cards on her first turn. Does she get to remove them from the game or not?

Empower Yourself

Self-Analysis, Strengths

Did you know that a person must have average or above-average intelligence in order to be diagnosed with a learning disability?

1. a) All the people featured in the article are intelligent, yet they were called names when they were young or they thought badly about themselves. Look back to the article and record the negative labels that were used by others or themselves. You may wish to record your thoughts on a chart like this one:

Person	Labels Others Gave Them	Labels They Gave Themselves

b) Now, think about your own friends or people you know at school. Why do you think people call each other names? Work with your whole class to brainstorm ideas, and record them on a chalkboard or on chart paper.

c) Why do you think people use bad labels about themselves? Work with your whole class to record your ideas on a chalkboard or on chart paper. You may wish to record your thoughts on a T-chart like this one:

Why People Call Others Names	Why People Call Themselves Names

d) In a group of two to five students, examine the class's responses. Are there any common responses? Are any of the reasons similar?

e) Review the article (pages 112–113) to find the strengths that each person has and make note of them. You may wish to record your strengths on a chart like this:

Person	Strengths

f) Take a minute to think about your own strengths. Maybe you show your greatest strengths outside school—for example, taking care of family members, cooking, or being good at a part-time job or hobby. You may wish to record your strengths on a chart like the one below. In your working group, go around the circle and let each member share one strength he or she has. Go around the circle a second time and let anyone who wishes add a second strength.

Our Group	Strengths

g) As a group, identify those strengths that anyone can develop to help them succeed in life. A positive attitude and a willingness to work hard might be two. You may wish to record your strengths on a chart like the one below:

Strength	How It Leads to Success

h) On your own, design a piece for your portfolio that demonstrates
   - your strengths today
   - the strengths you hope to develop in the future.

   Your piece could be a paragraph, a collage, a pamphlet, a poster, a Web site, or a PowerPoint presentation.

CHAPTER 7
Your Wired World

Urban Legends of the Internet

Connect the Text

- How do you know what is true and what is not?
- Have you ever seen pictures that you thought might be altered? How can you tell?

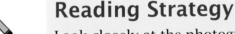

Reading Strategy

Look closely at the photographs and captions before you begin reading. As you read, look for the explanations that go with the photos. Then, return to the photos to understand how they were created.

What makes you believe something on the Internet? How do you know if something is true or not? 1

The Internet plays host to all kinds of stories and images. Some of them are true and some of them are false—or faked to seem true. Years ago, only professional photographers could **alter** a photograph. Today, because of digital photography, anyone can alter an image and invent a great story to go with it. Many of these stories and pictures become **urban legends**. 2

An urban legend is a modern story that is claimed to be true by the person telling it. These stories are **compelling** because they confirm our beliefs or biases, make us shiver, or warn us away from something. Urban legends play on emotions such as fear or the need to feel smug because we "know" something that others don't. Urban legends can never be **verified** and are always passed on by "someone" the storyteller knew. 3

Consider the photos on page 129. In one popular Internet story, the **critter** on the left and several other strange-looking fish were said to have washed up from the Indian Ocean during the tsunami of 2004. That fish story is fake but the photo is real. The fish and its cousins are actually examples of rare species found in the Tasman Sea, off Australia. However, linking this **menacing**-looking fish to the tsunami feeds people's fears more effectively. It also encourages them to pass the legend on. 4

How about the beautiful iceberg on the right? It has been used on the cover of several geography textbooks. Here is the urban legend to go with it, found on the Internet: 5

alter
change

urban legends
stories passed around that are said to be true

compelling
believable

verified
proven to be true by checking facts

critter
creature

menacing
dangerous-looking

J

1

Not washed ashore by the tsunami

The iceberg that wasn't

This is an amazing shot. This came from a rig manager for Global Marine Drilling in St. John's, Newfoundland. They actually have to **divert** the path of these things away from the rig by towing them with ships! Anyway, in this particular case, the water was calm and the sun was almost directly overhead so that the diver was able to get into the water and click this pic. They estimated the weight at 300 000 000 tonnes.

6

divert
move, change direction

Sounds picture-perfect, doesn't it? However, this image is about as fake as it gets. It is made up of four photographs shot in two different locations—Alaska and Antarctica. The underwater portion of the iceberg is really above water. That image was simply turned upside down and joined to the other image to create the right effect. The sky was also **imported** from another photo.

7

imported
inserted from another source

Celebrities are often the subject of urban legends because their lives seem so unreal. Years ago, when singer Mariah Carey achieved overnight success with a string of pop tunes, she became the target of an **unflattering** urban legend. Carey was quoted as saying, "When I watch TV and see those poor starving kids all over the world, I can't help but cry. I mean, I'd love to be skinny like that, but not with all those flies and death and stuff."

8

unflattering
causing someone to look bad

STAMP Out Bullying

> "Bullies are always cowards at heart."
> — *Anna Julia Cooper, teacher and writer*

Connect the Text

■ Do you think the above statement about bullies is true? Why or why not?

■ What are the different types of bullying?

Reading Strategy

Read the following list of words and predict the type of bullying this article discusses:

cyber	*Criminal Code* of Canada	freedom of speech
malicious	censorship	Web site

○○○ BullySTAMP : Home

http://bullystamp.com/ ▼ ◉ G▾

BullySTAMP   Home page   Search: [   ]   **Web Search**

BULLYSTAMP
STANDING TALL AGAINST MEAN PEOPLE

GO
HOME

POST
YOUR STORY

REPORT
A BULLY

GET
INVOLVED

KNOW
YOUR RIGHTS

Welcome to the BullySTAMP Web site! 1

This site is for people who want to stamp out Internet bullying. It's also to 2
help those of us who've been attacked online. Rather than turning away and
allowing these cowards to call us names and ruin our reputations, we're here to
say we're not running away or giving in.

That's where we got our name, BullySTAMP: Standing Tall Against Mean People. 3

It all began two months ago when someone from our school put up a 4
mean-spirited Web site about a friend. We won't mention names, but the
site was full of hurtful, false claims. Whoever wrote the comments stayed
anonymous, while our friend was made fun of. It may have seemed funny to
the bully, but it wasn't.

Our friend withdrew from school and his friends, hiding in his room while the 5
bullies had a laugh at his expense. The scary thing is, the attacks came out of
nowhere. He hadn't done anything, and suddenly there was a hateful Web site
about him full of lies. It could happen to anyone at any time.

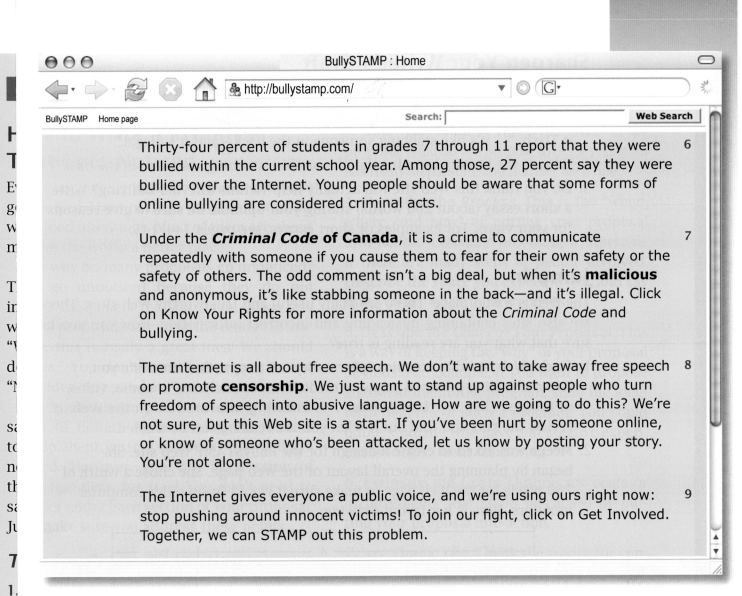

Thirty-four percent of students in grades 7 through 11 report that they were **6** bullied within the current school year. Among those, 27 percent say they were bullied over the Internet. Young people should be aware that some forms of online bullying are considered criminal acts.

Under the **_Criminal Code_ of Canada**, it is a crime to communicate **7** repeatedly with someone if you cause them to fear for their own safety or the safety of others. The odd comment isn't a big deal, but when it's **malicious** and anonymous, it's like stabbing someone in the back—and it's illegal. Click on Know Your Rights for more information about the _Criminal Code_ and bullying.

The Internet is all about free speech. We don't want to take away free speech **8** or promote **censorship**. We just want to stand up against people who turn freedom of speech into abusive language. How are we going to do this? We're not sure, but this Web site is a start. If you've been hurt by someone online, or know of someone who's been attacked, let us know by posting your story. You're not alone.

The Internet gives everyone a public voice, and we're using ours right now: **9** stop pushing around innocent victims! To join our fight, click on Get Involved. Together, we can STAMP out this problem.

mean-spirited
having mean feelings and intentions

malicious
acting in a way to hurt someone on purpose

anonymous
not revealing an identity

censorship
banning information or art

Criminal Code of Canada
Canadian laws about crime and punishment

Read for Meaning

1. For what audience is the BullySTAMP Web site intended?
2. What is the purpose of this Web site?
3. How is the word "STAMP" used in "BullySTAMP"? What is that usage called?
4. When is free speech a crime under the _Criminal Code_ of Canada?
5. On which tab would you click to describe your experience with a cyber-bully?
6. Provide words with the same meaning as the following:
   a) cyber   b) viciously   c) anonymous

Read for Meaning

1. Summarize the main points of Celine's and Marcus's essays in a graphic organizer like this one:

Use of IM-Speak at School

Celine Says NO	Marcus Says YES
1. Introduction (main point)	1. Introduction (main point)
2. Reason 1	2. Reason 1
3. Reason 2	3. Reason 2
4. Reason 3	4. Reason 3
5. Conclusion (main point)	5. Conclusion (main point)

2. What is the main idea of paragraph 2 of Celine's essay?

3. To whom is Celine talking when she says, "Stop talking about 'yrslf' and how 'u got' an opinion. Probably not."

4. Why did Celine's teacher penalize her for saying, "Probably not"?

5. Are the following statements made by Marcus facts or opinions?

   a) IM-speak is useful and not harmful.

   b) When the teacher is speaking, many students struggle to take everything down.

   c) Years ago, lots of people learned shorthand in order to work in an office.

6. According to Marcus, why do adults have a problem with IM-speak?

Sharpen Your Writer's Craft

1. Both Celine and Marcus end with a strong closing statement. Explain what makes each one effective.

2. With whom do you agree more, Celine or Marcus? Give a brief explanation for your answer, without copying from the text.

3. Write your own five-paragraph essay about any topic related to the theme of this chapter, "Your Wired World." Your teacher will provide you with support. Start by using **Line Master 7-9: Essay Planning Templates.**

How to Be Persuasive

Have you ever tried to persuade someone to do something? Then you know that persuasion is a skill.

Being persuasive means encouraging someone to believe as you do, or to act as you do—or both. Persuasion is not about bossiness or begging. It's about getting another person to see the situation as you do. Persuasion is sometimes called "winning the heart and mind."

Essays must be built with good arguments and good evidence (see Skills Workshop, page 115). However, arguments alone can be dry. Persuasion is what makes an argument believable.

How can you introduce persuasion into your essays? Here are some strategies.

Tips on Being Persuasive

1. Base Your Examples on Familiar Situations

Your examples should make people think, "That's so true. I've been in that situation!" Then, they will want to keep listening to you.

2. Talk about Fairness

Appealing to people's sense of fairness makes them want to agree with you. For example, in paragraph 2 of his essay, Marcus noted, "When the teacher is speaking, many students struggle to take everything down." This statement encourages readers to think about making the situation fair for all students.

3. Use Wit to Bring People On-side

That was Celine's intent when she said in paragraph 2, "J.K. Rowling and Roald Dahl never said ROFL." She knew that the image of these authors using IM-speak in their books would make readers laugh with her and possibly persuade them to agree with her.

4. Lead Readers Where You Want Them to Go

You can do this by using words such as "of course," "as a result," "yet," or "in fact." For example, in paragraph 4, when Marcus says, "*In fact*, they sometimes criticized our parents," he seems to understand the situation clearly, and you want to believe him.

Practise the Skill

1. In your next writing assignment, try to use at least one or two strategies to introduce persuasion.

   a) How did the strategies you chose make your writing better?

   b) How will you do things differently next time?

2. Create your own definition of "persuasion" in the form of a catchy phrase, such as "winning the heart and mind."

Jump In

Marcus has a hunch that IM-speak is a faster way of taking notes than writing out words in full. He has designed an experiment for the Science Fair to try to prove his hypothesis.

Marcus gave each of his classmates a 150-word e-mail written in standard English and asked them to copy it, either by typing it out again on a computer or writing it out in pen. Half of the students were asked to make their copy using IM-speak instead of standard English. Here is the plan of his experiment:

	IM-Speak		Standard English	
	Typing	Writing	Typing	Writing
Group number	1	2	3	4
Group size (students)	4	5	4	5

Marcus set up his experiment like this. How many students were typists? How many were writers? How many used IM-speak? How many used standard English?

Here are the results of Marcus's experiment:

Marcus's Results

Group Number	Time to Copy E-mail (in minutes)				
	Student 1	Student 2	Student 3	Student 4	Student 5
1	7.50	7.25	8.75	7.50	—
2	7.00	8.25	5.75	5.50	6.00
3	4.50	7.25	5.75	5.50	—
4	7.00	7.50	6.75	9.00	8.50

Group 3's challenge was to type in standard English. Here, Seth tries to beat his official test results of 5.75 minutes.

1. Find the average time to copy the 150-word e-mail for each group by adding the times in each group, and then dividing by the number of students in that group.

2. Find the copying rate in words per minute (WPM) for each group by dividing the number of words copied by the average times you found in activity 1, above. Round your answer to the nearest whole number.

3. Was Marcus's hunch right? In several sentences, explain what his results show.

4. Were typists faster than writers? Use Marcus's results to support your answer.

Empower Yourself

Analysis, Self-Reflection

1. In her essay, Celine states, "students will need to write standard English once they get a job or go to college." Do you find that lots of people give you advice or warnings about things you will need to do, or things to look out for in the future?

   a) As a class, brainstorm some of the common types of advice that older people give to teenagers. Keep the list in a public place so that everyone can refer to it.

   b) In a group of two to five students, think about advice that has been given to you in the past. Use a T-chart to create some examples of good advice that paid off, and bad advice that didn't work out so well.

   c) In your working group, discuss what makes good advice effective. Does it matter who is giving or who is getting the advice? Is timing a factor?

   d) Create a list of all the factors that influence giving good advice. You may wish to post your list or share it with the rest of the class.

2. In your group, imagine that you could stop an adult before he or she started to give advice to teenagers.

   a) What would you like that adult to keep in mind?

   b) Create a set of guidelines for adults in giving teenagers advice. You could create a check list, a top-10 list, or a handy tip-sheet.

   c) Share your guide with the rest of the class.

3. On your own, imagine that you could travel through time and speak to

   • your younger self in the past

   • your older self in the future.

   a) What advice would you give to your younger self?

   b) Write a paragraph, or create a graphic organizer, to explain the advice you would have given to your younger self. Make sure you explain why you needed advice and how the situation actually turned out.

   c) Write a second paragraph, or create another organizer, with advice you would like to give to your future self. Maybe you are considering different educational paths or different choices in life. What would you like to say to your future self about choices you are making right now? Keep this advice in your portfolio, and be sure to look at it from time to time.

PART 3

Explore Your Opportunities

In this section of *Learn Smart*, you will have the opportunity to

- find and record the information you need in a variety of situations
- plan school courses and identify graduation requirements
- learn the steps and strategies of self-advocacy
- communicate effectively to seek information and assistance or to advocate for yourself

- identify careers and volunteer opportunities that suit your interests and abilities
- make the most of your school and work portfolios
- create a resumé to enhance future opportunities

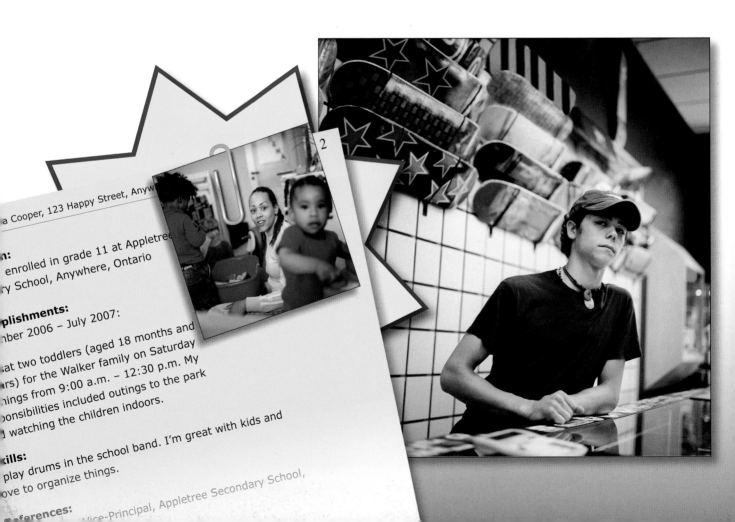

a Cooper, 123 Happy Street, Anyw

n:
enrolled in grade 11 at Appletre
y School, Anywhere, Ontario

plishments:
nber 2006 – July 2007:
at two toddlers (aged 18 months and
rs) for the Walker family on Saturday
hings from 9:00 a.m. – 12:30 p.m. My
onsibilities included outings to the park
d watching the children indoors.

kills:
play drums in the school band. I'm great with kids and
ove to organize things.

eferences:
Vice-Principal, Appletree Secondary School,

CHAPTER 8
Getting the Information You Need

The Winning Numbers!

Have you ever dreamed of winning the lottery? Imagine the scene: you and your family perched on the edge of the couch while you hold the ticket. One by one the numbers are called. You cannot believe it! Those are *your numbers*.

What's next? What steps would you and your family have to take to get your hands on those millions?

Not so fast! The Agulto family must figure out whom to contact before they collect their prize.

Stepping Stones to the Prize

Your parents probably remember which lottery they played. If they don't, you could remind them to examine the ticket. The name of the lottery will be prominently displayed on it.

Now, you must check the ticket for instructions on what to do next and for any specific rules. Your family needs this information in order to collect the prize. For example, if the prize is under $200, you may be able to collect your cash at a local convenience store. But if the prize is larger, you may need to contact the lottery itself.

How will you do that? It makes sense to look on the back of your winning ticket for the phone number and Web site of the lottery corporation. Then, you can telephone the organization or go online for further information. Lottery officials will tell your family to come to the lottery office with the winning ticket and some kind of identification.

How will you know what to do when you get to the lottery corporation? You could ask a receptionist to direct you to the right office. At the winnings office, someone will take your ticket and make you sign an agreement. For example, your family may have to agree to have their picture published in the newspaper. You're getting closer!

Throughout this process, notice how you and your family are always seeking new information. Not until you figure out how to claim that money will you get to spend it.

Jump In

1. Help 18-year-old Carmen get on the right path to collecting her lottery riches. She has just won second prize, but her instructions on collecting the cash are all mixed up. On **Line Master 8-1: Find the Right Order**, show the order that Carmen should follow to collect her prize. Write the number of the correct step in each stone from left to right.

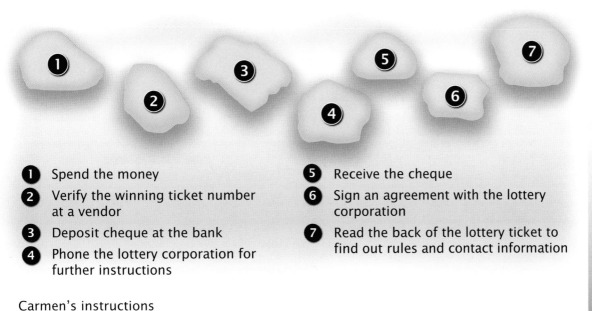

❶ Spend the money
❷ Verify the winning ticket number at a vendor
❸ Deposit cheque at the bank
❹ Phone the lottery corporation for further instructions

❺ Receive the cheque
❻ Sign an agreement with the lottery corporation
❼ Read the back of the lottery ticket to find out rules and contact information

Carmen's instructions

2. a) You have just won $1 million! Create a pie graph (see page 72) to show what percentage of your money you will spend on the following. Remember that your plan should make you a winner for life, not just a winner today.

- clothing
- travel and holidays
- charity
- electronics
- education fund
- savings and investments
- vehicles
- gifts for family
- other

b) Write a short paragraph about your pie graph. What did you spend the most money on? Why? What did you spend the least money on? Why? If you indicated a percentage for "other," describe what was in that category.

3. Reread the Wise Words on page 153. Is this good advice? Explain.

A World of Information

Figuring out how to collect lottery winnings is just one example of getting information from a **system** or organization. Here's another. Have you ever downloaded music to an MP3 player and organized a playlist?

A computer is an electronic system that operates using certain rules, just like the lottery corporation. There are specific steps to follow in order to download music.

system
several parts that work together as a whole, such as a computer operating system

Always download responsibly. Pay for your music, find free sources of tunes, or check out Web-based radio for unlimited listening.

Six Steps to Music Satisfaction

1. Identify "where the music is."

2. Access a music player (e.g., iTunes or Windows Media Player). This action gets you "in" to the system.

3. If you don't already know how to download, learn how. Select Help from the tool bar on the computer screen and follow the cues. You may find an index of topics, or the number of a tech support line. Or, simply ask a friend!

4. With your new knowledge, find the music titles you were seeking.

5. Now you can download, create playlists, mix songs, and more.

6. Enjoy the music!

Congratulations! You used a system to get the music you wanted to play.

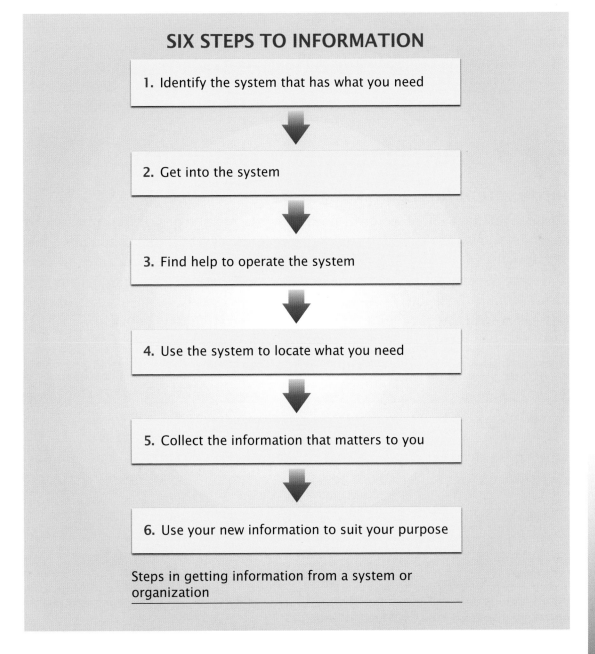

SIX STEPS TO INFORMATION

1. Identify the system that has what you need

2. Get into the system

3. Find help to operate the system

4. Use the system to locate what you need

5. Collect the information that matters to you

6. Use your new information to suit your purpose

Steps in getting information from a system or organization

WISE WORDS

It's not what you know. It's knowing where to look.

Jump In

Use **Line Master 8-2: My Need, My System** to show how the six steps of getting information (see the flow chart on page 155) can be applied to many systems and organizations.

First, define your need. Next, choose a system or organization from the list below. Then, fill in the details for the system you choose.

- bus/train/airline service
- movie theatre chain
- public library
- Google
- school guidance department
- tutoring service
- animal shelter

- counselling services
- gym
- Canada Post
- store chain
- provincial government
- band government
- police services

Example:

My need: "I have to get to Sarnia by 6 p.m. on Tuesday."

> 1. I identify the bus/train/airline service.

Information for You

Throughout this course, you will need to locate other types of information. For example, you will be expected to locate helpful resources in the community. You will also be expected to identify the academic requirements to graduate.

How will you get that information? The process will be similar to figuring out how to collect those lottery winnings or download music. In most cases, you will be dealing with the three kinds of information shown in the table below.

Written Information	Electronic Information	People Information (face-to-face or by phone)
• Books • Magazines • Brochures • Flyers • Guides • Maps • Tables • Photos and art • Billboards	• Web sites • E-mail • Blogs • Search engines • Collaborative or team site (wiki) • Help menu • Map program (MapQuest, Google Earth)	• Guidance counsellor • Tech support line • Teacher • Receptionist • Nurse • Librarian • 411 or "0" • Store clerk • Police officer

Information is available in different formats. Some of it is written down; some is available online; and some is held by people in organizations.

Jump In

Go on a hunt! Your task is to communicate with three different systems or organizations. You will come away with three different kinds of information—written, electronic, and people information. Your information should help you at school or should apply to one of your personal or career interests.

1. Choose the organizations you will approach. See Jump In, page 156, for ideas.

2. Figure out which kind of information you will get from each one—written, electronic, or people.

3. Follow the steps in the flow chart on page 155 to get your information.

4. Bring your written information to class—for example, a brochure or pamphlet.

5. Download and print your electronic information and bring it to class.

6. Record your people information and bring your notes or recording to class.

Here is what Rami did:

System	Written Information	Electronic Information	People Information (face-to-face or by phone)
MapQuest		I made a map of my home at 233 East Park Crescent for a friend	
Basketball coach			I asked the coach about vitamin supplements
Police	I got a brochure about the entry requirements for the Ontario Police College		

7. Now, recall a time at school when you had to gather information and you were dissatisfied with your results. How was your old system of information-gathering different from the six-step system? What is it about the six-step system that works for you?

Getting What's Yours at School

Your school is another type of organization. Its resources include

- the people who run the school, such as the teachers, principal, vice-principal, and support staff
- all the school's equipment, including classrooms, books, technology, sports facilities, and so on.

Your education depends on your ability to access and use these different resources. Your teachers are there to help, but it's your task to locate what you need.

First, you have to know how your school works. All schools are intended to work, but they are not all the same. Look at the diagrams below to help visualize your high school's organization.

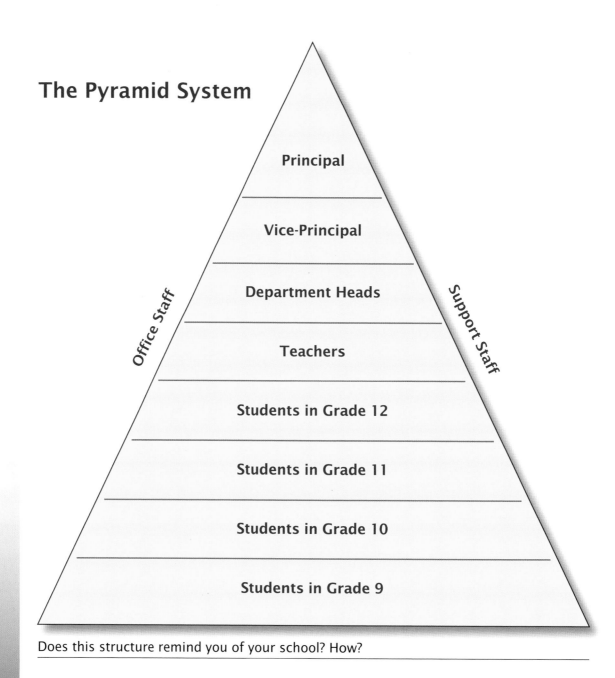

The Pyramid System

Principal

Vice-Principal

Department Heads

Teachers

Students in Grade 12

Students in Grade 11

Students in Grade 10

Students in Grade 9

Office Staff

Support Staff

Does this structure remind you of your school? How?

The Cell System

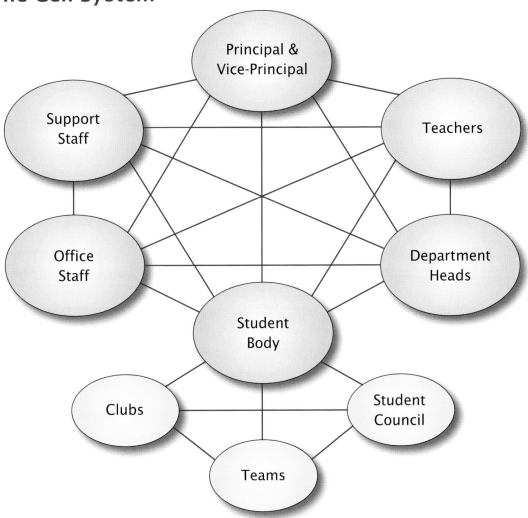

Does this structure remind you of your school? How?

_____

Jump In

One way to understand your school's organization is to meet people at different places within the organization.

1. Using **Line Master 8-3: School Interview Form**, interview at least three people in three different positions:

   - principal
   - vice-principal
   - teacher
   - department head
   - member of office staff

   - member of support staff
   - student council member
   - student club or team member
   - student club or team head

2. What kind of organization does your school have—pyramid or cells? How does that organization affect the way you go about getting information?

What You Need to Graduate

Selecting courses to match your strengths (see Chapter 1) and knowing about graduation requirements will help you get on the path to success.

Selecting Your Courses

The key to course selection is having a plan. You need to know

- what courses you must take in order to graduate (**required courses**)
- what courses lead to more advanced courses (**prerequisites**)
- what courses you could take to suit your strengths and interests (**options**).

There may be a special time to select courses. To help you decide which courses to take, your school may offer a booklet or a Web site that describes course offerings. Sometimes you will be asked to input your course selections directly into a computer program.

A teacher or guidance counsellor may also be available to answer your questions. Don't be afraid to ask them for what you need. This is an example of accessing the resources at your school the way you would at any organization. (Go back and review the Six Steps to Information on page 155, and also see Chapter 9, page 175, about advocating with teachers.)

Jump In

1. Use the information you collected about yourself in Chapter 1, including your "smarts," your preferred learning style, and your interests. This information will be located in your portfolio. Now, think about what you would really like to study. This is not a question you need to answer in five seconds. Mull it over. Ask other students or a teacher for their input.

2. Examine
   - the Ontario Ministry of Education requirements at **www.emp.ca/ls**. This list will tell you the credits you must earn in order to graduate.
   - other courses you could take (options) to suit your strengths and interests. Find this information in your school booklet or on the school's Web site.

3. Now, try filling out a table like the one below. (Your school may have its own template that you can use.) This table applies only to your next year. Later, you will have the chance to plan courses in one subject area all the way up to grade 12.

My Courses Next Year		
Required Courses	**Optional Courses**	**Prerequisites**
English		
Math		
Science		
Canadian History		
Canadian Civics (half course)		
Careers (half course)		

4. A non-academic requirement to graduate is 40 community service hours, such as volunteer work.
   a) What types of volunteer work do you do or have an interest in doing?
   b) List examples of volunteer work you noticed in this chapter and in other sections of *Learn Smart*.
   c) How could you best plan to accumulate these hours between now and graduation? Tip: See Chapter 2 for ideas on goal-setting and using your agenda.

Imagine Your Future

Now that you've thought ahead to the next year, try to imagine beyond that time. What jobs would suit your strengths and interests?

Business and Retail
- good with people
- skilled in math
- trend watcher
- good communicator
- decision maker

Education
- interested in kids
- excited by learning
- strong in academics
- able to plan ahead

Health and Science
- detail oriented
- able to master facts and procedures
- a people helper
- calm under pressure

What Do You Need to Be In ... ?

Sports
- fit
- physically well coordinated
- disciplined
- competitive
- a team player

Trades
- good communicator
- analytic and creative
- problem solver
- well coordinated
- happy working alone

The Arts
- creative
- disciplined
- able to sell yourself
- able to cope with rejection
- comfortable taking risks

Justice and Advocacy
- good with people
- good advocate
- able to reason
- honest and responsible
- respectful of the law

Jump In

1. Joel wants to work at a home supply chain for a few years after graduation. This large chain sells building materials, home supplies, tools, and appliances to homeowners and tradespeople. It's a place where customers ask a lot of questions, and all the salespeople must be knowledgeable about the merchandise. Joel is currently in grade 10.

   a) What skills would help Joel in this job? Why?

   b) What secondary courses would help him? Why? Think about all three types of courses—required, prerequisite, and optional.

   c) Working back from the grade 12 courses, follow the prerequisites to see what Joel would need to study next year. Rank these courses in order of importance.

2. Now, follow the same process with a field of your choice, such as sports, business, or justice. Use **Line Master 8-6: Examples of Jobs** to find specific jobs in a general career area. Place your information in your portfolio. Check your information regularly to keep track of what you wish to study and what you have studied.

Community Resources to Support Learning

Sometimes you need help outside school. Maybe you want extra help with a difficult subject, or you want to develop one of your interests.

Who helps outside school? Many students work with a **coach** or instructor to develop an area of interest, such as sports or music. Others use a **tutor** for different subjects. Many students find this one-on-one contact helpful because that person listens to them and gives them specific help based on their needs.

Getting assistance outside of school helps you in school. You learn even more strategies for success.

coach
someone who trains and encourages you in a skill or sport

tutor
someone who helps you with a specific school subject

A tutor can work inside or outside school and can often help you with a specific need.

When Nick Needs Help

Nick had to face it—he was bombing math. He didn't like to fail, but this was different. He couldn't fail any course. If he did, his parents wouldn't let him play on the rep hockey team. They offered to pay for a tutor, but it was up to him to find one.

How will Nick go about finding a tutor? Nick can start at the school guidance office. Staff there will let him know what help is available. Some schools offer **peer tutoring**, where strong students work with those who need extra help. Some schools also offer after-school help provided by teachers.

There are other places Nick could go to get help from the community. A tutor or a community youth centre are two examples. A tutoring service will offer help in a variety of courses. However, some of these services can be expensive. Local community centres often provide mentors or volunteers who can help with schoolwork, counselling, or interests such as sports or other activities. These services may be free or may be covered by the cost of membership.

Nick could access any of these resources. How? He'll use the basic "six steps" you learned about on page 155. He will

- identify the system that has what he needs
- get into that system
- get help finding his way around the system
- locate the person who can help him
- get the help that matters to him
- use this help to improve his school performance or lifestyle.

Jump In

1. Do you have what you need from the community?

   a) Go on a community scavenger hunt. Based on what you have read about accessing organizations in the community, identify five things you want or need. Here are some examples.

Wants and Needs	Type of Assistance	Example
Mental	Subject-related help (e.g., in math, English) from a teacher, tutor, peer helper, or mentor	Sergei gets tutoring in English twice a week because English is not his first language.
Physical	Sports instruction at a gym or community centre, or instruction in activities such as dance, yoga, crafts	When her local community centre offered tap and jazz lessons, Allison signed up with a buddy.
Emotional	Help with emotional issues from a school counsellor, doctor, or social worker, or through a help line	Suzanne meets with a school counsellor weekly because of stress related to her parents' divorce.
Social	Help getting involved with student clubs, interest groups, online communities, or volunteer activities	Anton joined the chess club and now competes with his team against other schools.

b) Pick one need or want you have in each of the four main categories—mental, physical, emotional, and social. Double up on one category.

c) Now, pick your top need or want from your list. Using the basic "six steps" on page 155 and **Line Master 8-7: Community Resources Scavenger Hunt,** find out

- what services are offered
- where the services are located
- when these services are available
- how much they will cost.

2. Once you have accessed and used one service, answer the following questions:

a) How has that service contributed to your school success?

b) How has that service contributed to your physical or emotional well-being?

Place your completed **Line Master 8-7** and your answers to activity 2 in your portfolio.

This chapter introduced you to the following ideas:

- Through your actions, you can find and access the information you need.

- The "six steps" to accessing any system (or organization) are:

  1. identifying the system that has what you need

  2. getting into the system

  3. finding help to operate the system

  4. using the system to locate what you need

  5. collecting the information that matters to you

  6. using the information to suit your purpose

- There are three kinds of courses—required, optional, and prerequisite. These are described on page 160.

- Knowing the requirements to graduate is the responsibility of all students.

- There are many community-based resources to help enhance learning. These are described on page 163.

CHAPTER 9
Be Your Own Advocate

What Is Self-Advocacy?

Does it appear to you that some people are always lucky? They always get what they want and things always seem to go their way.

Maybe they are not lucky; maybe they are just excellent **advocates** for themselves. Self-advocacy means

- knowing yourself and knowing what you need
- knowing who can help you
- being able to ask someone for what you need.

To be a good self-advocate, you must be able to do all three things.

advocate
(noun) someone who speaks out in support of something or someone

(verb) to speak out in support of something or someone

STEPS TO SELF-ADVOCACY

1. You need something

2. You realize that someone has what you need

3. You ask for help in an appropriate way

Everyone needs help at some time! Sometimes you need to ask a teacher for extra help at school. Sometimes you need to ask a friend for a ride home. In both of these situations, you are using self-advocacy skills.

Jump In

1. The word "advocate" can be either a noun or a verb. Look this word up in a dictionary.

   a) Use the word "advocate" in a sentence that clearly shows it is a noun.

   b) Use the word "advocate" in a sentence that clearly shows it is a verb.

2. a) With a partner, brainstorm situations when you might have to advocate for yourself with

   • a teacher

   • an adult in the community

   • your classmate

   • someone in another situation.

   Write down those situations. You can take rough notes for this part of the activity.

   LM 9-1

   b) Select three of your examples and transfer them to a table like this one:

Situation	What I Want	The Best Place to Meet	How I Would Prepare

LM 9-2

3. You have identified three examples of times when you could advocate for yourself.

   a) Carefully think about each situation and decide how important it is to you.

   b) Rank-order each example from 1 to 3, with number 1 being the most important to you and number 3 the least important.

   c) Compare your rank-ordering with that of a partner. How are they the same? How are they different?

Why Self-Advocacy?

Maybe you find it easier to speak up for other people than to speak up for yourself. Of course, it is good to help others. However, it is equally important to be able to help yourself. Being able to help yourself is not selfish—it is the right thing to do.

Imagine you are standing in line at a fast-food restaurant in front of someone who is older and taller than you. The cashier looks right past you and says, "Can I help you?" to the other person.

What do you do?

If you say nothing, you may go without lunch. You may become angry. Perhaps you feel that grumbling loudly will get the cashier's attention. However, if you advocate for yourself, you can resolve your problem more quickly. All it takes is saying, "Excuse me, I am next in line." That is the power of advocating for yourself.

Jump In

1. Look at the drawing above.

   a) List two other effective things the girl could have said or done in this situation. Why are they effective?

   b) List two *ineffective* things the girl could have done in this situation. Why are they ineffective?

2. Is being a self-advocate worth it? Take time to reflect and respond.

Self-Advocacy Strategies

Students who advocate for themselves may do so in a variety of situations. But they always come prepared with a **strategy**.

Some ways to be prepared are to

- make a list of what you need
- practise what you are going to say to the person
- have a back-up plan to deal with "bumps."

strategy
a way to plan something

WISE WORDS

Luck is when opportunity meets preparedness.
— *Old saying*

Strategy 1: Make a List

Making a list helps you think about what you want to ask for. It also helps ensure that you have covered all the points you want to make. Number your points so that you can re-read your list or refer to any point easily.

If you are describing a problem, your list could take the form of the "Five W's" (who, what, when, where, and why). That way, you give your listener a quick overview of the problem without focusing on one detail.

At the end of your discussion, it is a good idea to say, "I think I have covered all the points I want to make, but just let me check my list." Then, do your check. If there is an important point you have not yet covered, raise it now.

Strategy 2: Practice Makes Perfect

Rehearse what you are going to say by role-playing with a friend or parent or by practising in front of a mirror. This will help you hear what you sound like. It will also help you imagine how the other person might respond to what you are saying and how you are saying it.

Strategy 3: The Back-up Plan

What if you get nervous or angry, or the other person doesn't seem to respond? You need a strategy to keep yourself going. It can be as simple as having a water bottle handy so that you can pause to take a drink. Pausing will let you focus on your goal, not on your nervousness or anger. After you have had a sip of water, return to one of your points.

Jump In

1. a) Find an example of an advertisement in a magazine or newspaper that you like. Cut out the ad or photocopy it and attach it to your notebook.

   b) Answer the following questions in your notebook underneath or beside the ad:

      i) What product is the ad selling?

      ii) According to the ad, why should you buy the product?

      iii) Is the message conveyed in words or images, or both? Explain.

      iv) What does the ad tell you about the product? What else about the ad makes this product appealing?

      v) Would you buy this product? Why?

      vi) If you could give the creator of this ad advice, what would you tell him or her?

LM 9-3

2. Now you're going to sell self-advocacy! Create an advertisement for the print media (e.g., a magazine, newspaper, or billboard) to sell self-advocacy. Your ad should be 15 cm × 20 cm, and it must

   • convince consumers that they need self-advocacy

   • explain how self-advocacy will help make their life better.

   Tip: Review the questions and answers from activity 1b), above, to help you create a good advertisement.

How to Reflect on Your Actions

Reflection is the skill of taking time to think about what you have done. At school, you are sometimes asked to reflect on how you have learned and how that learning can help you.

You may think that your life is too busy for reflection. However, even the busiest people understand its value. Professional sports teams always watch a tape of the game they just played the next day. Why? Because they are looking at what they did right and what they did wrong so that they can improve their performance.

In school, reflection sometimes looks like correcting your work, but it is really much more than that. There are three important questions to ask yourself when reflecting:

- What?
- So what?
- Now what?

Try this guided reflection about self-advocacy. Your teacher will assist you.

Remember a time when you had to advocate for yourself, *or* a time when you wish you had but didn't.

What happened? Make dot-jot notes outlining the events. Re-read your dot-jots. Do you have any other points to add after re-reading? If you do, add them.

Next, ask yourself, **"So what?"**

- What could you have done that you didn't do?
- What could you have said that you didn't say?
- Do you know someone who handled this situation in a way you admire? What did he or she do?

- Can you use this person's example to help you?
- Who could give you advice with this situation?

Now what? Imagine this situation happening again. List three things that you would do differently this time. What do you think will happen because of your actions? Read the following three quotations. Choose one and explain how it applies to your situation.

"All people make mistakes, but only the wise learn from their mistakes."

— *Winston Churchill*

"Take chances, make mistakes. That's how you grow."

— *Mary Tyler Moore*

"Anyone who has never made a mistake has never tried anything new."

— *Albert Einstein*

Athletes' performances are often filmed or photographed. That way, they can watch what they did and improve their performance next time.

Knowing Whom to Approach

Complaining to your friends or whining about a situation is not advocating for yourself. People who advocate for themselves don't sulk—they take action by approaching the right person. The right person is always the person who can actually do something for you.

It's always a good idea to start as close to the issue or problem as possible. For example, if you feel a teacher has not marked your paper fairly, approach that teacher first, not the principal. In this situation, the teacher can give you what you want—your paper re-marked!

Why is sulking the opposite of self-advocacy?

Jump In

Imagine yourself in each of the situations below. Identify whom you need to approach and what you will be asking for. You could place your answers in an organizer like this one:

LM 9-4

Situation	Person to Approach	What I Ask For

1. You asked your supervisor at work if you could have the long weekend off. However, when the schedule is posted, you are scheduled to work all day Saturday.

2. The third-base coach waves you home and you get tagged out. The team manager yells at you and tells you that it's your fault the team lost the game.

3. The school secretary calls you to the office to say that your older brother dropped off your lunch. She tells you to stop forgetting your lunch and says your brother disrupts the office by playing delivery person.

4. Your teacher has assigned groups for a major project. You know that the other members of your group never take their work seriously.

Who's Your Audience?

Your audience is the person (or persons) whom you are approaching. The more you know about that person, the better. Ask yourself:

- What do I know about this person?
- What is important to that person?
- How should I approach him or her?

The father of Matt's friend Jayesh Patel runs a landscaping business. Matt would like to ask Mr. Patel for a summer job. Mr. Patel has told Matt to e-mail him to set up an interview. Examine the e-mails below. Which one do you think will get Matt the interview? Why?

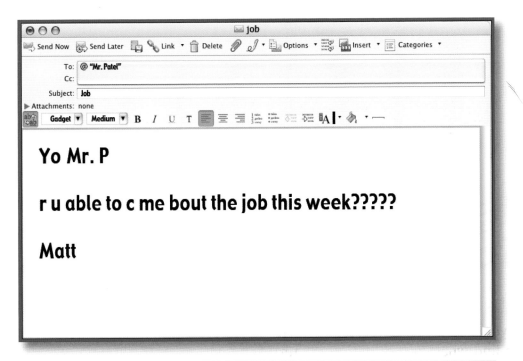

Who is the audience for Matt's e-mail? What impressions is Mr. Patel receiving about the sender in each example? How will these impressions affect his decision?

Knowing your audience is also important when you are in a difficult situation and need help. When you approach someone, ask the same three questions: What do you know about that person? What is important to him or her? What kind of approach should you take?

Jump In

Writing an e-mail is different from having an online conversation with someone. Depending on the person you are writing to, your e-mail will have a certain style.

1. Write a short (one- or two-sentence) e-mail for at least three of these situations.
   - You want your friend to bring your jacket to school that you left at his house.
   - You want to tell your grandmother about a good mark you got in school.
   - You want to ask a friend to go to the movies on Saturday night.
   - You want to ask the woman that you babysit for if you can use her name as a reference on your resumé.
   - You want to tell your teacher that you will be away on Friday because your hockey team is in a tournament.

2. Review the situations above and the e-mails you have written.
   a) Which of these situations are examples of self-advocacy? Explain why.
   b) Which of these situations are *not* examples of self-advocacy? Explain why.

Tips for Advocating in Different Situations

Most people like to help others. In fact, knowing how to make people feel good about helping you is an important part of self-advocacy.

You will find that people appreciate it when you

- call them by their name
- look at them directly
- speak in an **assured** but polite tone of voice
- thank them for their time, or acknowledge the help they have given.

assured
confident, not afraid

Those are the basics. But body language is also important—it should support your message. Try to sit or stand in a way that shows you are interested in what the other person is saying. You should look as though you are giving the conversation your full attention. (See Skills Workshop: Making Body Language Work for You, page 60.)

Body language that says you're pleasant and confident will go a long way.

Jump In

Review the drawings on page 59, your answers to activity 3 (all parts) (page 59), and the Skills Workshop: Making Body Language Work for You (page 60). These examples demonstrate communication without words—body language.

1. Create a list of behaviours that would demonstrate negative body language in a self-advocacy situation—for example, looking at your watch or the clock while the other person is speaking.
2. Create a list of behaviours that would demonstrate you are serious about your issue. For example, if the teacher meets you after class and you've sat at the back of the classroom, you can move closer to the teacher so that neither of you has to yell.

Advocating with Teachers and School Administrators

As a student, you may have to advocate for yourself with a teacher. Remember that teachers are busy people. Find out when that person will be free and make an appointment to meet that person. Scheduling an appointment sends a signal to a teacher that you are serious about your issue and that you respect the teacher's schedule, too.

Taking the time to find out when and where your teacher would like to meet shows respect and maturity.

Getting Past Bad Experiences

Not all people are the same! Just because you had one bad experience doesn't mean that everyone you approach will act the same way. Keep a positive attitude, and show the next person that you really believe in your request.

Jump In

1. Role-play one of the scenarios listed on **Line Master 9-5: Self-Advocacy Scenarios**. Prepare to meet with the teacher to discuss your situation and make your request. Prepare by answering the following questions. See page 169 for additional help.

   a) How will you ask this teacher to meet with you?

   b) What will your main points be? Make a list.

   c) Imagine you are the teacher. Write down three questions you think your student will ask you. Prepare the answers to those questions.

   d) What will you do to make the teacher feel good about meeting with you?

   e) What will your back-up plan be if you get nervous or angry?

   f) Write down the type of body language you want to use with your teacher.

2. With a partner, role-play your scenario from activity 1, above. Your partner will play the teacher and you will play the student. In your role-play, demonstrate effective self-advocacy.

3. Imagine that you want to go to a friend's house in another town for the weekend. You must ask your parents for permission.

   a) Create a list of questions that your parents might ask you before they grant permission.

   b) How does creating this list of questions help when you are self-advocating?

All in the Timing: When *to Advocate*

It is important to understand when to advocate. Sometimes it is necessary to speak up immediately. At other times, it's wise to wait and plan what you are going to say.

If you feel angry and you need to compose yourself, take some time to calm down. However, if your own safety and well-being are at stake, you must speak up immediately—for example, if you found yourself in an unsafe situation on a job site.

Jump In

In "Be Your Own Counterfeit Detective" (pages 38–39), Saahir received and tried to spend a counterfeit bill. Timing was everything; because Saahir advocated for himself, he was able to get out of a difficult situation. Knowing when to self-advocate is an important skill. Practice will help you make the decision with confidence.

1. Create an organizer similar to the one below.

Situation	Saahir accused of passing fake $20 bills
Advocating Now: PROS	• was able to convince manager he didn't know it was fake • would look guilty if he walked away • could explain where and how he got the bill • knew to speak politely and not lose his cool
Advocating Now: CONS	• manager might not believe him, might get him into trouble • wasn't able to ask for any advice • didn't know if he could get his $$ back • might blow up at the manager … would make him look guilty!
Now or Later? Why	Advocate now because he can't walk away without looking guilty
Partner's Response	*Agreed. Saahir had to tell his story immediately so it didn't look made up.*

2. Identify four situations in which self-advocacy may be necessary. You may use some of the examples from page 174 of this chapter or make up your own.

3. For each situation, determine the pros and cons of advocating immediately.

4. Then, decide whether you should advocate immediately or wait. Include the reason why.

5. Share your situations and responses with a partner. Does he or she support your decision? Why or why not? Your partner should complete the last row of your organizer, as in the illustration above.

 LM 9-6

Advocacy Support Groups

A support group is a loose network of people to call on for advice in different situations. Family members or friends can be a part of your support group; so can classroom teachers, homeroom teachers, special education teachers, or guidance counsellors. Look for people who can help you to

- identify your needs
- plan strategies to advocate for yourself with others.

A good support group can not only give you advice—its members can also help you role-play or practise. People in your support group are there to help you reach your goal.

Jump In

1. Take a few minutes to think about the following questions:
   - Do you have a support group?
   - Do you know who your support group is?
   - From whom have you asked advice in the past?
   - Did you like their advice? Why?

   a) Make a list of qualities you believe people in a support group should demonstrate.

   b) Prioritize your list of qualities by rank-ordering them from 1 to 5, with number 1 being the most important.

   c) Complete an organizer like the one below. First, list the people who could help you with different types of issues. Next, identify the type of support or advice they could provide. Place this list in your portfolio.

Person	What type of advice can he/she provide?

2. a) Choose *one* of the following resolutions and conduct a debate:
   - "I don't need a support group because I have lots of friends."
   - "A good self-advocate does not need a support group."

   b) Write a journal entry about the debate.

   c) Were you surprised by the results of your debate? What would you do differently next time? How is a debate similar to self-advocating?

Careers in Advocating on Behalf of Others

There are many opportunities to advocate on behalf of others. Some of these opportunities are paid jobs. Others are volunteer opportunities.

Child and youth advocates protect the rights of children in difficult situations such as family break-ups or **domestic violence**. Youth advocates also protect young children's rights at school.

- Social workers advocate for families. They help to find them support services and may advocate for them in court. Social workers also advocate directly for students aged 16 and over.
- Lawyers advocate for their clients in court. In some countries, lawyers are called *advocates.*
- Lobbyists advocate for groups of people who need protection, such as low-income families, people with disabilities, or young employees. They speak to different levels of government on their behalf.
- Ontario also has a Child and Family Service Advocacy Office, which is part of the provincial government. It advocates for the rights of children and youth under 16 years of age.
- Special-education teachers advocate for students with an IEP. (For more on IEPs, see Chapter 10, page 196.)

domestic violence
violence and abuse (such as hitting, punching, name-calling) in the home

Canadian basketball star Steve Nash high-fives a young fan during a charity event in Toronto. Nash raises money to provide services to children affected by poverty, illness, abuse, or neglect.

Jump In

1. What is the difference between paid advocacy and volunteer advocacy? Do you think one is more important than the other?

2. Is Steve Nash a paid advocate or a volunteer advocate?

3. *Learn Smart* has introduced you to many advocacy groups, such as War Child Canada, Free the Children, Make Poverty History, and the Children's AIDS Health Program. There are many others.

   a) List as many different advocacy groups as you can think of. Use the four already mentioned to get you started.

   b) Choose an organization that you feel passionate about and would like to join.

   c) Use **Line Master 9-9: Internet Site Data Collection Form** to gather information about your chosen organization.

4. a) Using the information from **Line Master 9-9**, write a two-paragraph opinion piece about why someone you know should also support this organization. Your audience can be almost anyone, including a family member, teacher, or friend. (For models of longer opinion essays, see pages 144–145.)

   b) Find a picture that illustrates some aspect of your organization. Write an original caption for the picture. Include this picture as part of your opinion paper.

5. Find five want ads for jobs. You may use either the newspaper or the Internet.

   a) What type of information does the ad contain?

   b) Identify five types of information that are common to all the ads.

   c) Now, create a job ad for a paid advocate. Be sure your ad contains the five types of information that you identified in activity 5b).

6. Would you consider taking a job as a paid advocate? Why or why not?

This chapter introduced you to the following ideas:

- Self-advocacy means

  - knowing yourself and knowing what you need

  - knowing who can help you

  - being able to ask someone for what you need.

- Self-advocacy is not about being selfish; it's about being able to help yourself.

- When you advocate for yourself, it's a good idea to have some strategies. These include making a list of the points you want to talk about, practising beforehand, and having a back-up plan.

- Always know your audience—it will help you refine your message.

- It's important to choose the right time to advocate for yourself. Sometimes it's better to speak up right away. At other times, it's better to let things cool down.

- A support network can help you figure out when and how to advocate for yourself.

- There are many careers in advocacy, including social work and law.

- There are many volunteer opportunities to advocate on behalf of other people.

CHAPTER 10
Portfolios That Work

Pictures in My Pocket

Geoff was so excited about his trip to a local television station that he couldn't wait to show his pictures around. When he got home, he laid them out for his friends: watching the warm-up for their favourite show; operating the camera; shaking hands with the host; visiting the editing suite and learning about all the equipment.

Geoff also told some great stories about his day, but what really impressed his friends were the photos. It was obvious that everything Geoff described really happened.

Have you ever been in Geoff's situation? When your friends asked you for more details about "what actually happened," how did you respond? How many ways can you think of to record "what happened" so that you can show others later?

In the control room with Bob.

Helped operate the camera for this shot!

Down Memory Lane

Christen is a collector of memories. A couple of times every year, Christen takes all her pictures, concert ticket stubs, menus, cards, and e-mails—anything she has saved over the last few months—and puts them into a scrapbook. Her scrapbook includes not only these **artifacts**, but descriptions as well. Some of her descriptions are quite short, for example, a date or a person's name. Other descriptions go into great detail about what happened, what she thought, or how she felt.

When Christen and her friends look back on an event, her scrapbook tells the story. Her friends always find that the evidence in Christen's scrapbook triggers more memories and more enjoyment, too.

Scrapbook or Portfolio?

Christen and Geoff have something in common; they both have evidence—records that support their stories and memories. You probably have this kind of evidence, too. Collecting evidence such as pictures or artifacts helps you remember your past and stay connected to it. It also shows you where you are today in relation to yesterday.

The same is true of school evidence—all the work and the assignments you produce throughout the year. At school, your collection of assignments and other work is not called a scrapbook; it's called a **portfolio**. Evidence collected for a portfolio is the story of your learning. It helps you track your progress.

Jump In

As a class, discuss the following:

1. What do you collect?

2. How do you organize your collection?

3. Why do you use that method of organization and not another?

artifact
anything made by people

portfolio
collection of work that displays your learning and experience to others

Why a Portfolio?

A portfolio has many uses:

It is the place where you gather all the evidence of your learning.

It is the place where you can see where your learning came from. How were you thinking, and how did you approach assignments and problems? What progress have you made?

It holds your first drafts as well as your polished pieces of work.

It may be a requirement for a specific class.

It is often the basis for conferencing with your teacher, or it may be used during parent–teacher conferencing.

It can even leave school with you, if you plan well.

Throughout this course, you have been adding to your portfolio on a weekly basis. In this chapter, you will learn how to make it serve you well in other settings, such as getting a part-time job, winning a spot on a team, or transferring to another school.

Jump In

Examine all the ways to use a portfolio presented on these two pages.

1. Which ways have you tried?

2. Which ways haven't you tried?

3. Identify one new way to use your portfolio based on the suggestions on pages 184–185. Give a reason for your choice.

Portfolio Purpose and Audience

Much like a scrapbook, a portfolio is selective. It holds what is useful and what is "best." As a collection of documents, it supports the stories of your past achievements. It is a way to prove what you say when talking about your learning.

Unlike a scrapbook, a portfolio targets a larger audience than just you and your friends. Figuring out your portfolio's **purpose** and **audience** at any given time is the key to using it well.

purpose
what you expect to do or achieve

audience
the people hearing your message

Your Portfolio	
What's the Purpose?	**Who's the Audience?**
Requirement for a specific class	you, teacher
Requirement for an assignment	teacher, other students
Focus for discussion on parent–teacher interview night	you, parent
Personal record of your school successes	you, parent, peers
History of your learning and participation in extra-curricular activities	school clubs, teams, community programs
Document to bring to a job interview	potential employer, parent with a job lead

Matching the purpose of your portfolio with the intended audience will help you get it right. On the following pages, you will have the opportunity to brush up on your portfolio skills with two different purposes in mind. You will

- assess the value of an existing school portfolio or develop a new one
- create and manage a portfolio for career-related activities.

The School Portfolio

You are already maintaining a portfolio for your learning strategies course. It's safe to assume that you will create other portfolios for other classes throughout high school.

Remember: a portfolio may be worth a grade that will contribute to your overall average. Moreover, it is useful because it organizes the evidence of your thinking and learning.

School Portfolio Check-up

Welcome to your portfolio check-up! Are you getting the most out of your portfolio? Consider the four steps to great portfolios.

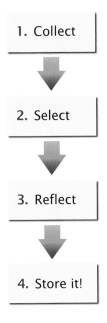

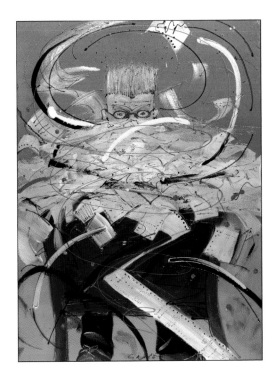

Stuff without order is just stuff.

Step 1: Collect

What work belongs in a school portfolio?

Some portfolios end up being great collections of "stuff." They contain interesting and useful things, as well as work you are proud of. However, you may not know exactly what's there. Would you allow your photo albums, scrapbooks, or playlists to get so disorganized?

One way to bring order to an unruly portfolio is to divide it into sections:

- a section for teachers, parents, and peers—your "public"
- a private section just for you.

As you collect material for your portfolio throughout the year, keep this organization in mind. It will help you weed out things that don't belong and help keep your material organized.

A Portfolio Assignment

Christen and Geoff take the same learning strategies class. The newest class assignment:

> Keep track of your work in English and mathematics for the past semester. Place the evidence of your learning in your portfolio, and bring it to parent–teacher interview night at the end of the month. Present your portfolio as evidence of your learning.

Christen and Geoff groaned when they heard this assignment. Christen had been faithfully collecting and organizing material, but she didn't think she had learned much in either subject that semester. What would she do? Geoff was doing well on his tests and assignments, but he realized he didn't have any proof. His organization was a disaster!

Mentor to the Rescue

Christen and Geoff talked as class was getting out. Geoff's brother Jamel was in grade 12 and had kept several portfolios during high school. He was now putting the finishing touches on a work/postsecondary portfolio. Geoff said he would ask Jamel for help.

Geoff and Christen caught up with Jamel in the library. They needed help!

Jamel agreed to mentor both Christen and Geoff for their portfolio assignment. He started by asking, "What did the teacher ask for? Look at the assignment sheet. Usually, it has all the instructions on it."

Then Jamel asked some questions. They sounded familiar! Pretty soon, Jamel, Geoff, and Christen had a master plan for the portfolio assignment. It looked like this:

Jamel's Question	Sounds Like	What We Know (assignment sheet)	What We Could Do
Why are you making this portfolio?	Purpose	We're supposed to show our learning in English and math during the last semester.	Look at our notebooks and review the major things we learned. Select the work that shows what we learned.
Who's going to look at it, and why?	Audience	It's for the teacher to use with our parents during interview night.	We want to include our best work. The work should show what we've achieved. Maybe include drafts in math?

Locating the Evidence

In English class, Geoff and Christen had produced the following:

- a descriptive paragraph
- an example of clear instructions
- a dialogue to show conflict between two characters
- a summary

They had also edited and revised their work.

In mathematics, they had spent most of the semester on problem solving using perimeter, area, and volume.

The pair set about locating their work in these areas. The assignment was clear: it said to select their very best work. Christen felt much better about the assignment already. She remembered what she had learned that term, and she had lots of work to choose from.

Geoff, however, was concerned about locating all his work. Then he got this e-mail from Jamel:

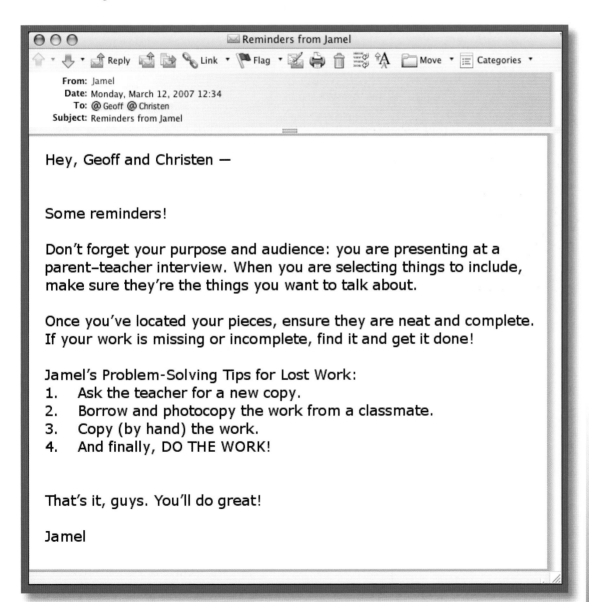

From: Jamel
Date: Monday, March 12, 2007 12:34
To: @ Geoff @ Christen
Subject: Reminders from Jamel

Hey, Geoff and Christen —

Some reminders!

Don't forget your purpose and audience: you are presenting at a parent–teacher interview. When you are selecting things to include, make sure they're the things you want to talk about.

Once you've located your pieces, ensure they are neat and complete. If your work is missing or incomplete, find it and get it done!

Jamel's Problem-Solving Tips for Lost Work:
1. Ask the teacher for a new copy.
2. Borrow and photocopy the work from a classmate.
3. Copy (by hand) the work.
4. And finally, DO THE WORK!

That's it, guys. You'll do great!

Jamel

The Day Arrives

Here are some examples of completed assignments that Christen and Geoff picked for their portfolios. They enjoyed discussing each piece. As they discussed their work, they talked about

- the challenges of learning some of the material
- how their understanding grew over the term
- their pride of achievement
- how what they learned could be useful in the future—for example, in a career.

The evening was a great success!

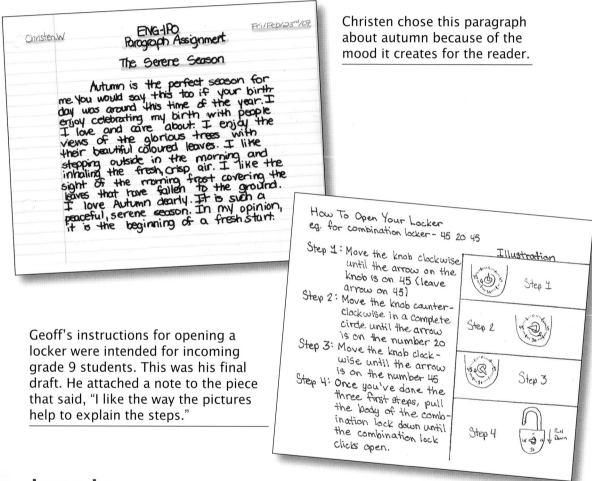

Christen chose this paragraph about autumn because of the mood it creates for the reader.

Geoff's instructions for opening a locker were intended for incoming grade 9 students. This was his final draft. He attached a note to the piece that said, "I like the way the pictures help to explain the steps."

Jump In

Christen and Geoff did their portfolio assignment. Now, it's your turn.

1. Review the work you did in any course during the last term.

2. Select the best evidence of your learning.

3. Try replacing one piece of lost work using Jamel's Problem-Solving Tips for Lost Work (page 191).

4. Present your portfolio pieces to a partner role-playing a family member.

5. What did you learn through this activity about the value of maintaining your portfolio?

How to Find a Mentor

Everyone can use a mentor. A mentor is a guide—someone with more experience in your area of need or interest. Mentors can

- share their experiences with you
- let you bounce ideas off them
- support you in your goals
- assist you with your challenges
- present you with options or different ways of looking at situations.

Although mentors may have lots of experience, they are not there to boss you around. Nor are they supposed to provide you with all the answers. Ideally, a mentor should make you feel more inspired about your own life and work.

So, where do you find this great person?

Tips on Finding a Mentor

1. Find Out If Your School Has a Mentoring Program

Some Ontario schools train older students in coaching and mentoring. These students are paired with younger students who want to be mentored. Find out whether your school has such a program.

2. Identify What You Want to Get Out of Mentoring

This will help you narrow the field. If you want to know more about a career interest, select someone with that interest too. Talk to your school's co-op teacher, student success teacher, or guidance counsellor. They might be able to refer you to someone in your community who can mentor you at school.

If you want help in resolving an ongoing conflict, you should look for someone who has managed conflicts before. Does your school have older students who have been trained in conflict resolution? Is there an elder in your community who could take on this role?

3. Use Your Personal Connections and Networks

Look around. Who's doing what you would like to be doing—and doing it well? You could start by approaching that person and asking for a small piece of information.

Once you've made the first approach, ask yourself:

- Did that person have the information I was looking for?
- Did he or she share information easily?
- Was he or she a good listener?
- Would I feel comfortable asking that person to talk to me again?

4. Approach Your Local Service Organizations

Many Lions Clubs, Rotary Clubs, and Knights of Columbus chapters offer mentoring talks and youth mentoring at school. Contact your local chapters of these organizations to find out more information.

A mentor is a guide, not a boss.

The Beyond-School Portfolio

A portfolio can leave school with you. It can help you obtain summer employment or a part-time job. You might also use a portfolio to get into another school or community program. This kind of portfolio is referred to here as a "work portfolio."

What goes into a work portfolio? At the very least, a work portfolio should include your

- **resumé** and
- **references** or **letters of reference**.

Resumé Check-up

Use this section of the chapter to check out your knowledge of what goes on a resumé.

A resumé tells the person reading it who you are. It is like a snapshot of your experience, schooling, accomplishments, and skills. It is usually necessary to have a resumé when you apply for a job.

Personal Information

On your resumé, you must include information about where you live and where you can be reached. Generally, this means your

- name
- street address
- e-mail address (optional)
- telephone number.

Education

Your resumé should tell the person reading it how much schooling you have had. State what grade you are in or have just completed. Mention any courses you have taken outside school.

A resumé can match you with the right opportunities by presenting you in the best light.

Accomplishments

You can list your accomplishments on your resumé. Think about any teams you have played on, school activities or clubs you have joined, jobs you have held, volunteering you have done, or awards you have won. These do not have to be "big" things—they could include babysitting jobs or helping a neighbour. Usually, it's important to let an employer know that you handle responsibility well.

Remember that it's not enough to say you "played on a team" or "volunteered." You should give all the details you can, including names, when these activities occurred, and what you actually did. You could also include a picture, if it shows your activities clearly.

Example:

Education:
Currently enrolled in grade 11 at Appletree
Secondary School, Anywhere, Ontario

Accomplishments:
September 2006 – July 2007:

Babysat two toddlers (aged 18 months and
3 years) for the Walker family on Saturday
mornings from 9:00 a.m. – 12:30 p.m. My
responsibilities included outings to the park
and watching the children indoors.

Skills:
I play drums in the school band. I'm great with kids and
love to organize things.

References:
Ms. Wiseman, Vice-Principal, Appletree Secondary School,

Skills

A skill is an ability to do something well. You can state your skills on your resumé
and provide proof in the form of finished work drawn from your school portfolio.
Don't forget your outside-of-school skills, such as swimmer levels, first-aid quali-
fications, or music training.

What if you wanted to show that you were a good communicator? You could
state that fact on your resumé and include some school documents—such as written instructions or a letter to the editor—as proof.

Other skills to highlight on a resumé might include

- being a leader
- being a good problem solver
- having great organizational abilities
- having good computer skills.

References

These are the people who will vouch for your experience and say favourable things
about you. Remember: they should be able to talk about the qualities that the person reading your resumé wants to know you have. These qualities might include
being a team player, or being polite, punctual, and dependable.

Do your references know you well enough to say these things about you?

Jump In to Your Resumé

So you found a part-time job you want to apply for! All applicants must submit a resumé. What do you do?

1. Your job is to create a resumé or revise an old one. Use the sample resumé on page 195 as a model, and each part of the Resumé Check-up on pages 194–195. If you have to approach anyone for additional information to include on your resumé, refer to the self-advocacy tips in Chapter 9 on page 174. Include your

   - personal information
   - accomplishments
   - skills
   - references (names)
   - letters of reference.

2. Dorinda has highlighted her problem-solving, time-management, and organizational skills on her resumé. Identify a piece of evidence for each skill that would prove Dorinda possesses that skill. For example, she was a team leader on a specific project last term and managed everybody's time and responsibilities well. This evidence could come from school, her volunteer work, or a part-time job.

Options in the Work Portfolio

You could also place any of the following items in your work portfolio.

Transcripts

A transcript is a written record of your grades from the time you entered a school. Copies of transcripts are given to students upon request. Many postsecondary schools require them.

IEP (Individual Education Plan)

If you have an IEP, keep a copy in your portfolio. It lists your strengths and needs, and it legally supports your right to any **accommodations** in the classroom. Your IEP also includes information on moving to a postsecondary program.

accommodations
what a school must do for certain students to give them equal opportunities to learn

Timetables and Schedules

These remind you of how much time you actually have to plan your life beyond school. What will you do today?

Postsecondary Programs

If you have located information about postsecondary programs related to your career of interest, you could keep that information in the work portfolio. This would include both information about requirements and application forms.

Letters of Reference from Teachers

These will be useful to you, whether you transfer to another program or seek summer employment. For tips on obtaining a letter of reference, see page 195.

Interviews

If you have interviewed for a job, you could write up how the interview went and place the information here. Even if you feel it did not go well, it may be useful to include. For example, you could write down the questions you were asked. That way, you can review what took place and improve your performance the next time.

Performance Reviews

When you get more job experience, you may get a performance review. If your review is positive and mentions some of the skills you want to highlight, add the review to your work portfolio.

Interview go badly? Feel disappointed? Don't be. There's always a next time. Write down what you weren't prepared for. Be prepared next time.

Jump In

1. Find and acquire your school grades from the guidance office or main office at your school.

   a) Check both offices to find out where your transcripts are located.

   b) Make a copy of your transcripts to include in your portfolio.

   c) Create a set of instructions for other students wishing to obtain their transcripts. Your set of instructions should include the following information:

      • where the transcripts are located

      • whom to ask for assistance

      • photocopying procedures (who does it, and where?)

      • cost, if any

      For examples of written instructions, see pages 116 and 192.

2. Zenia had an interview at a pet supply store. The woman who interviewed her asked what she knew about the different breeds of dogs and small animals sold at the store. Zenia said she didn't know anything about them. She thought she would be selling pet food and equipment to people who already knew what they wanted. She didn't get the job. Worse, the interviewer laughed at her as she left the store.

   a) Was it appropriate for the interviewer to laugh at Zenia? Why or why not?

   b) What should Zenia do now?

   c) Do you think Zenia needs to know something about animals in order to work at the shop? Why or why not?

   d) How could she find out this information?

   e) How could Zenia use this experience to get ready for the next job interview?

   f) What information about this experience could she store in her portfolio?

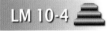

This chapter introduced you to the following ideas:

- A portfolio holds the evidence of your learning. It backs up what you say about what you know.

- There are different uses for a portfolio. These are described on pages 184–185.

- Portfolios have different purposes and audiences. These are described on page 186.

- The four steps to great school portfolios are: collect; select; reflect; and store it!

- A work portfolio includes, at the very least, a resumé with references.

- A work portfolio can also include other items related to your education, work experience, or career interests. These items are described on pages 196–197.

- A resumé includes your personal information, education, accomplishments, skills, and references.

- A mentor is a guide who can help you with one or more of your areas of need or interest. Tips on locating a mentor can be found on page 193.

PART 4
From Here to There

In this section of *Learn Smart*, you will have the opportunity to

- apply your *Learn Smart* knowledge and skills to other school situations
- imagine using your new knowledge and skills after graduation

CHAPTER 11
Four Doors

"So, now what?" you may be asking. You've learned a great deal in this course. But new knowledge and skills aren't worth very much unless you can apply them in a variety of situations.

Knock, Knock

Knock on these four doors and find the situation that fits you best. Then, use the steps provided to guide you through the process.

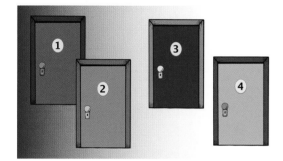

Come prepared, not stressed, at exam time.

Door Number 1

Your learning strategies course has ended, and next month you will be facing exams. You have two weeks to do all your preparation. Where do you start?

1. Ask your teacher for an exam outline in each subject area. This outline will be your guide to *what* to study.

   a) Read the exam outline carefully. What do you understand well? What do you need to review or learn again?

   b) Make a list of the areas that need your attention under each subject. Record everything on **Line Master 11-1: Study Plan by Subject**.

SUBJECT: GEOGRAPHY		
What I Know Well	**What I Know to Some Extent**	**What I Don't Know**

summary
shorter version of longer text that includes the key ideas

index
an alphabetical listing of the main topics and subtopics of a book with page references

glossary
a listing of key terms with definitions

2. Get out any class notes you have kept in each subject area. Review your notes and ask yourself the same questions for each subject: What do you understand well, and what do you need to review or learn again? Add anything else to **Line Master 11-1**.

3. Locate your textbooks in each subject area.

   a) Check the chapter introductions and **summaries** against your exam outline and take note of pages where information can be found. Is there anything else you need to add to **Line Master 11-1**?

   b) If you are unsure about how important an idea is, check to see whether it is mentioned on your exam outline, and look in the textbook's **index**.

   This is a sample index entry from *Learn Smart*:

   > brain
   >   analytic, 5
   >   creative, 5

   Locate the pages where the idea is found. Make sure you have noted them.

   c) If you run across a term you don't know, check it out in the book's **glossary**.

4. Now you're ready to create a study schedule using **Line Master 11-2: Exam Prep Timetable**. Your schedule should let you spend the most time on the material that you don't understand, or that you know only to some extent.

   Use the information found in The Five-Day Countdown: Test Preparation Plan (page 22) to help you plan your days on each subject area. Remember, most of your time for the next two weeks will be spent studying, so you can probably review a few subjects each day.

5. Now you're ready to study. Turn to the Skills Workshop: How to Homework without Sweating on pages 20–21. Review points 3 and 4 on your study space and preferred learning style.

6. If you are missing class notes, make them now while you study. Writing notes may help you retain the information. You can

   • borrow a classmate's notes as a starting point

   • make your own notes by picking out one key piece of information on relevant pages of your textbook.

   You can write or word-process your notes, or write each key idea on a sticky note and place it on the textbook page on which the idea appears.

   Remember to concentrate on the material that you don't know well or know only to some extent (as you recorded on **Line Master 11-1**). Finally, check the notes you are making against your exam outline. Are you studying what you should be studying?

7. When you've gone through all your subject areas once, go to day 3 of The Five-Day Countdown: Test Preparation Plan on page 22 and work through the rest of the plan (days 3–1) with each subject area. At this stage, you write down the most important information from each subject in the fewest words possible. If you have time, repeat any step you feel you need to.

Troubleshooting

Having difficulty reading or studying? Try the following tips:

- When reading the textbook, try using some of the reading strategies you have been introduced to in *Learn Smart*. You will find these strategies on pages 32–144, at the start of each article.
- Identify any study distractions and deal with them. For tips on dealing with distractions, see page 25.
- Figure out whether you are procrastinating. For tips on avoiding procrastination, see page 23.
- Consider working with a peer or professional tutor for a few days. You can find information on peer and professional tutors on pages 163–164.
- Stressed? Check back over the healthy lifestyle tips on pages 26–28.

Door Number 2

You are interested in using your new knowledge and skills in other classes. Where do you start?

Apply your learning to new situations.

1. Make a list of the learning situations in other courses that can challenge you. (Tip: You may find some of your personal challenges documented in your *Learn Smart* portfolio.) Call it your Top Five Learning Challenges. An example might be that you have trouble concentrating when someone is talking. Or, maybe you get bored during teamwork.

2. Once you have created your list, go to the *Learn Smart* index and try to locate all the information you can on your situation. Pay attention to the entries on learning, learning skills, learning strategies, smarts, motivation, interest, time management, and self-advocacy.

3. Now, write yourself a self-help manual for your Top Five Learning Challenges. Your manual should

- state each challenge you have chosen to focus on
- list the tips and solutions provided in *Learn Smart*, along with the relevant page numbers
- state how *you* are going to handle the situation the next time it comes up. What strategy will you choose? Why does it work for you?

I'm always going to use the 7 steps for problem-solving when I have a math problem. When I use these steps to work through the problem, I have a better chance of solving it. I also get less frustrated.	Skills Workshop: How to Solve a Problem, page 104

Door Number 3

You have a very specific goal: you want to assess how well you're doing in some of the basics. Where do you start?

Check your know-how in English and mathematics.

1. Try these summative activities in English and mathematics. A summative activity is not a small task. It is one that includes several important ideas and skills. It is intended to give you an accurate picture of how you are doing in different subject areas.

   Three different levels of difficulty are provided. You and your teacher can decide which level you should try.

   - **Line Master 11-3: English 1**
   - **Line Master 11-4: English 2**
   - **Line Master 11-5: English 3**

   - **Line Master 11-6: Math 1**
   - **Line Master 11-7: Math 2**
   - **Line Master 11-8: Math 3**

Door Number 4

You are focused on graduating or participating in a work-study program. You are mostly concerned about using your skills in the real world. Where do you start?

1. Start with your *Learn Smart* school portfolio. Go back to the sections that document your abilities and interests. Remove that information and examine it carefully.

2. Go back over the following activities: Jump In, activity 3a), page 53; Empower Yourself, page 55. What did you learn about your career possibilities, based on your abilities and interests? Also, locate any career-related information you have in your portfolio.

3. a) You are about to meet your own personal job coach. This person's only purpose is to help you get a great job. Your task is to write a letter to that person outlining your job goals. In your letter, refer to the evidence you gathered about yourself in activities 1 and 2, above. How are your job goals a good match with your abilities and interests?

   b) You are going to include a resumé with your letter. Update your resumé by following the guidelines in Chapter 10, pages 194–195.

4. Alternative to activity 3:

   a) You are about to meet with your own personal postsecondary coach. This person's only purpose is to help you get into the postsecondary institution of your choice. Your task is to write a letter to that person outlining your postsecondary goals. In your letter, refer to the evidence you gathered about yourself in activities 1 and 2, above.

   b) You are going to include a resumé with your letter. Update your resumé by following the guidelines in Chapter 10, pages 194–195.

5. To prepare for your interview with the job or postsecondary coach:

   • review the Skills Workshops on listening (page 9) and body language (page 60)

   • re-read these sections of Chapter 9: pages 173–175

6. Get your work portfolio ready for the interview in case your coach asks to see it. Go back to pages 196–197 to review what you can include in your work portfolio. Is there anything missing that you would like to include now? Then, do the work!

Use your new knowledge and skills in the real world.

GLOSSARY

A

abhor
hate, despise

abused
mistreated in a physical or emotional way

accelerates
increases in speed over time

accommodations
what a school must do for certain students to give them equal opportunities to learn

activists
people who work for a cause

addicted
emotionally or physically dependent on someone or something

ADHD
disability that makes paying attention and thinking things through difficult

advocate
(noun) someone who speaks out in support of something or someone; (verb) to speak out in support of something or someone

agenda
a tool for organizing your time by day, week, month, and year

AIDS
a serious disease that makes it difficult to fight infection

alter
change

alternative
something else you can choose

animation
putting pictures together to create the appearance of motion

anonymous
not revealing an identity

anti-retroviral medication
medicine for the treatment of infections such as HIV

artifact
anything made by people

assured
confident, not afraid

audience
the people hearing your message

B

block
refuse communication with (online)

brainstorm
to suggest ideas quickly

C

celebrity endorsement
statement by a famous person that a product is excellent

censorship
banning information or art

coach
someone who trains and encourages you in a skill or sport

cold turkey
quitting altogether, without tapering off

compelling
believable

conventions
accepted ways of speaking, writing, or doing

counterfeit
an imitation meant to pass as real; fake

***Criminal Code* of Canada**
Canadian laws about crime and punishment

critter
creature

cup
1 cup = 0.2 litres

currency
money that is in circulation today

D

data
information

debris
what is left over after something has been broken up

debut
first-time appearance

deforestation
large-scale cutting down and removal of trees

delegates
representatives picked by others to attend a meeting

demographic group
people who are roughly the same age and have similar interests

development organization
a group that helps poor countries improve their situation

dimensional weight
length times width times height, divided by 6000

divert
move, change direction

dividends
rewards or benefits resulting from efforts

documentaries
films about real people and events

domestic violence
violence and abuse (such as hitting, punching, name-calling) in the home

doodling
drawing without much thinking

doping
using drugs to improve performance in a sport

downloadable
able to be received over the Internet

dyslexic
has difficulty reading print

E

engineers
people who apply science to human needs

entrepreneur
a person who starts his or her own business

exclusive
a story broadcast or published by just one source

exotic
unusual and mysterious

e-zine
Internet magazine

F

famine
extreme shortage of food

floods of suds
high drama, as found in TV soap operas

foray
entrance into

fuel
substance burned for energy

full throttle
with the gas pedal to the floor

G

genocide
mass killing of people belonging to a race or nation

global hectare
average per hectare of the earth's renewable surface

glossary
a listing of key terms with definitions

goals
things you want to achieve

graphologists
people who analyze the meaning of handwriting

Greenpeace
international environmental organization founded in Vancouver, BC, in 1971

guru
an expert guide; someone who knows a lot about a particular subject

H

hail
lumps of ice that form in a storm cloud and drop to the ground

harnessing
directing the force of

HIV
the virus that causes AIDS

horsepower
a common measure of power

huddle
gathering of the team to go over the next plays

hurricanes
bad storms with a wind speed of at least 119 km/h

hyperactive
easily excited; has difficulty sitting still

I

imported
inserted from another source

impromptu
without advance preparation

index
an alphabetical listing of the main topics and subtopics of a book with page references

intelligence
the way a person understands

L

learn smart
to learn in a way that suits you; to maximize your strengths and manage your challenges

learning disability
disability that often involves spoken language or print

learning strategies
ways to help you learn more easily and effectively at school and throughout life

learning styles
three main ways to learn—through sight, hearing, or touch

lectured
told what is right for them

legend
colours or symbols used on a map

letters of reference
letters of support written by people who know you and your abilities

likeminded
two or more people who share a common belief

luxury
something rare and expensive; something nice to have that is not needed

M

malicious
acting in a way to hurt someone on purpose

malnutrition
state of not being properly fed; lacking protein and vitamins

manipulated
changed; influenced for a selfish purpose

marathon
any very long event

mean-spirited
having mean feelings and intentions

menacing
dangerous-looking

metaphor
literary term in which something is called something else for effect

meteorologists
people who study and forecast the weather

microprinting
printing technique that uses tiny print

mind games
acting in a way to confuse or manipulate someone

mood swings
extreme changes in mood; e.g., from happy to sad

N

nutrition
energy from food

O

online
on the Internet

options
courses you can take to suit your strengths and interests

P

peer tutoring
help from another student with studying or homework

perspectives
viewpoints; ways of seeing things

pesticides
substances used to kill plant, animal, and insect pests

pledges
promises to pay based on a unit (hour, kilometre)

portfolio
collection of work that displays your learning and experience to others

postsecondary
after high school

prerequisites
courses that lead to more advanced courses

procrastinating
avoiding a task by putting it off until later

purpose
what you expect to do or achieve

R

randomly
without any pattern

reason
understanding an idea because of another idea

references
the names of people who can vouch for the facts in your resumé

required courses
courses you must take in order to graduate

resilience
the ability to bounce back from difficulties

resumé
a document that summarizes your education and experience and is used to obtain a job

ROFL
IM-speak for "rolling on the floor laughing"

S

savvy
practical knowledge; hands-on know-how

scale
representation of distance on a map

scandal
a public incident that shocks people

shorthand
a method of speedwriting still used in some offices

silent treatment
not speaking to someone to show anger

sprinter
an athlete who runs short distances at very fast speed

standard English
the way that English is written in books and most other media

standard of living
quality of life measured by the goods and services enjoyed

staple
everyday item you use

strategy
a way to plan something

stress
forces acting on the body from the inside or the outside

subconscious
an active part of your mind that you are not aware of

summary
shorter version of longer text that includes the key ideas

surveillance
close observation of a person or group

suspicious
assumes bad things about someone or something

sustain
keep supporting

symbols
meaningful images that stand for other things

system
several parts that work together as a whole, such as a computer operating system

technical terms
terms of specialized knowledge, such as metaphor, perimeter, amoeba

tested positive
got a test result that showed use of a banned substance

THC
chemical that makes you high and reduces inhibitions (feelings that hold you back)

thesaurus
a dictionary of synonyms and antonyms

tornadoes
strong windstorms with funnel clouds

tournament
competition

training range
65–75 percent of your maximum heart rate based on your age

tread
walk

trend
movement in a certain direction; e.g., prices go up or they go down

tutor
someone who helps you with a specific school subject

ultraviolet
on the light spectrum, so violet that humans cannot see it

unflattering
causing someone to look bad

untouched wilderness
an area with no development

urban legends
stories passed around that are said to be true

V

vandals
people who destroy public property

verified
proven to be true by checking facts

veterans
people who have served in their country's military

W

wetsuits
diving suits

wheel horsepower
how much power is needed to move a car on a surface

window
an opportunity

INDEX

CREDITS

Legend: t = top; b = bottom; c = centre; l = left; r = right; CP = Canadian Press Photo.

Network website content courtesy of the Aboriginal Peoples Television Network, Winnipeg, Canada, © 2007: 31(br), 68; Recipe submitted by Verona/www.Allrecipes.com: 108; Australian Government/ Department of the Environment: 129(l); CP/Chris Bolin: 45, 48; CP/Adrian Wyld:179; Children's AIDS Health Program/www.LetsStopAIDS.org: 121; Corbis/ImageShop: Cover; Corbis/Design Pics: viii(bl), 1 facing, 25; Corbis/Simon Marcus: xi, 99; Corbis/Ole Graf/zefa: 4; Corbis/Tim Pannell: 9, 23; Corbis: 10, 175, 204; Corbis/Charles Gordon: 20; Corbis/Don Hammond/Design Pics: 27; Corbis/Gary Edwards/ zefa: 30(l), 100(l); Corbis/Zave Smith: 30(c), 100(r); Corbis/Tom Stewart: 31(tr), 50, 65; Corbis/Jim Reed: 32, 33; Corbis/Comstock: 38, 95; Corbis/Reuters: 39, 51, 90; Corbis/Rob Melnychuk: 43; Corbis/ Bettmann: 44; Corbis/Morgan David de Lossy: 61; Corbis/Earl and Nazima Kowall: 63(l); Corbis/Jack Hollingsworth: 71; Corbis/Kelly Redinger/Design Pics: 78; Corbis/Martin Philbey: 82; Corbis/Image 100: 84, 201; Corbis/DLILLC: 86; Corbis/Charles Gullung/zefa: 106; Corbis/Tom Shurtleff/Icon SMI: 113(l): Corbis/Frank Trapper: 113 (r); Corbis/Kevin Dodge: 115; Corbis/J.P. Moczulski: 120; Corbis/ Jack Hollingsworth/Blend Images: 127; Corbis/Ralph Clevenger: 129(r); Corbis/Playboy Archive: 138(tl); Corbis/Image Source: 142; Corbis/Jose Luis Pelaez Inc./Blend Images: 144, 147; Corbis/Estelle Klawitter/zefa: 145; Corbis/Randy Faris: 148; Corbis/Vera Berger/zefa: 149, 203; Corbis/Mika/zefa: 150(l), 194; Corbis/Helen King: 150 (r), 195; Corbis/H. Schmid/zefa: 151(t); 160; Corbis/Thinkstock: 151(b), 163; Corbis/Martin Ruetschi/Keystone: 154; Corbis/Mike Watson Images: 157, 190, 193; Corbis/ Pixland: 166, 197; Corbis/Robert Recker/zefa: 172; Corbis/Gareth Brown: 174; Corbis/John Lund: 182(r); Corbis/Steve Starr: 183; Corbis/Images.com: 187; Corbis/Normal/plainpicture: 200; Corbis/ Erik Freeland: 205; Epizootics.com: 74, 76; Flickr.com: 182(l); Paul Galpern: 109, 123; GO Transit: 103; Derek Grant: 80, 81, 171; Health Canada/canada.gc.ca/foodguide: 26; Hemp Products website: 83; Hotel Rwanda: 107; Howstuffworks Express: 30(r), 31(bl), 56(all); Rich Hulina Aviation Photography: 70; iStock photo: 28, 91, 110(both); London Police Service: 96, 97; Eric Oddleifson/New Horizons for Learning: 6; Used with the kind permission of the Spirit Bear Youth Coalition: 86-87 (essay), 89; War Child Canada: 31(tl), 63(r), 64(both); War Child Canada/Erin L. Pryde: 62(both); Tara Wells: 116(both); David Pike: 141.

Page 109: With thanks to Levi Sayers, Patrick Bois, and Joel Lanauze; produced at Queen Elizabeth District High School, Sioux Lookout, Ontario, as a project in Paul Galpern's Grade 11 Media Arts class.

Page 123: With thanks to Jasmin Libler, Rochelle Martin, and Justin Dennison; produced at Queen Elizabeth District High School, Sioux Lookout, Ontario, as a project in Paul Galpern's Grade 11 Media Arts class.

Page 192: Portfolio products created by students at Queen Elizabeth District High School, Sioux Lookout, Ontario, as a assignment in the Grade 9 Applied English class. Christen's season paragraph by Christen Wesley; Geoff's locker instructions by Darien Binguis. We thank teacher Michelle Ketchabaw, and all students who submitted written work.